Mind WorX

An Inside Story

DAN BRAND

BALBOA
PRESS
A DIVISION OF HAY HOUSE

Copyright © 2014 Dan Brand.

All rights reserved. No part of this book may be used or reproduced by any means, graphic, electronic, or mechanical, including photocopying, recording, taping or by any information storage retrieval system without the written permission of the publisher except in the case of brief quotations embodied in critical articles and reviews.

Balboa Press books may be ordered through booksellers or by contacting:

Balboa Press
A Division of Hay House
1663 Liberty Drive
Bloomington, IN 47403
www.balboapress.com.au
1 (877) 407-4847

Because of the dynamic nature of the Internet, any web addresses or links contained in this book may have changed since publication and may no longer be valid. The views expressed in this work are solely those of the author and do not necessarily reflect the views of the publisher, and the publisher hereby disclaims any responsibility for them.

The author of this book does not dispense medical advice or prescribe the use of any technique as a form of treatment for physical, emotional, or medical problems without the advice of a physician, either directly or indirectly. The intent of the author is only to offer information of a general nature to help you in your quest for emotional and spiritual well-being. In the event you use any of the information in this book for yourself, which is your constitutional right, the author and the publisher assume no responsibility for your actions.

Any people depicted in stock imagery provided by Thinkstock are models, and such images are being used for illustrative purposes only. Certain stock imagery © Thinkstock.

Printed in the United States of America.

ISBN: 978-1-4525-1381-2 (sc)
ISBN: 978-1-4525-1382-9 (e)

Balboa Press rev. date: 04/07/2014

CONTENTS

Acknowledgements vii
Preface ix

Two Worlds 1
Creation 58
The Library 79
Virtual Reality 105
The Amiable Reaper 156
Black Holes 165
Multiplicity 175
The Naked Taboo 198
Being Human 219
The Time Warp 302
Reflexions 308

Epilogue 329

ACKNOWLEDGEMENTS

FIRSTLY I'd like to thank my close family. A lifetime shared with them has taught me so much about life. I'd especially like to thank my son Troy, my daughter in law Kareen and their beautiful son Anakin, my one and only grandchild who is the joy of my life. Also my late son Clint, who died in 2001 of cancer at the young age of 27 years; the pain of his death, although devastating, taught me a great deal about the fleeting impermanence of life.

My mother Lorna, the sounding board for all my thoughts about life, my sister Sandra, who is probably the most avid reader of my work; also my brother Ken and his lovely partner Haley for their generosity, love and support; and to the rest of my extended family that are just too many to mention.

I'd also like to acknowledge everyone else who has ever crossed my path. All those many others that have played such an important role in my life story, the good, the loving, the sweet, the funny, the serious, and also the horrid and bloody hard to get along with.

Their footsteps have accompanied mine at one time or another along the same pathway of life and the interactions I have had with each and every one of those diverse human beings has taught me many very important lesson, not that I didn't find some of those lessons difficult to learn and accept, but unbeknownst to them, they, my loving family, my friends and adversaries, have all played a vital role in the writing of this book.

PREFACE

THIS book is really a number of short stories that has been compiled over a period of years, not only by reading, watching and listening to many renowned authors who are also seeking for answers, but from my life experience itself. So they don't necessarily flow from one to the other, although sometimes they do, but rather they are a random selection of topics that are separate and yet connected to the one theme: "What's life all about, who are we and why are we here?"

From an early age I've always been a seeker. Even when I was young I looked under the rocks and stones of life, curious to find out what was there, and more importantly, why it was there. Most people are content to live their lives with no thought about the world that surrounds them, and then there is some like you and I, that are inspired to seek for answers to the truth about who we truly are and why we are here.

We are the spice in the soup of life, the ingredients that make it more exciting and addictive. We, the questioners of life are essential components that make for a better recipe. On our shoulders lies the responsibility for man's continuing evolution. If you are reading this, then you are part of that group that has the curiosity and propensity to learn something new.

It only takes the few of us to be curious enough to probe the mysteries of life. Our fellow humans, who decide not to ponder the reasons why, will naturally follow in time, for the rising tide of learning lifts all boats.

Difficult questions such as, 'Is the world I experience around me real? Are the people around me real? Am I real? Or am I and everything else in this world just a part of some elaborate illusion, a dream conjured up by a Supremely Intelligent Energy (God)?

You will not find any answers to those questions in this book. I simple give my point of view on the possibilities of what might be, sign posts to the truth you could say. It's up to you the reader to discern what the truth might be.

It is best not to believe what is written here, for that would only put the damper on your learning altogether, but rather absorb the reasoning hidden between the lines. Then mix that reasoning with the ideas percolating in your own mind and come up with your own personal version of what reality may be.

That's a very important thing for you to do, for combined with the ideas that are emanating from the minds of the rest of us seekers of truth, man as a whole can then evolve and advanced to where we are destined to eventually be. So come on an entertaining and enthralling journey through the thoughts in my mind and see if I can plant a few fertile thoughts in yours.

TWO WORLDS

WE feel very much at home in the physical world that surrounds us, especially this planet we live on. We know it well, after all we were born here, all of the places we have ever been, all of the people we have ever loved or known are here, all of our lifetime experiences that make up the beliefs about who we are and what our life is all about was forged here in the furnace of the physical universe.

We work and play in it every day and each night we sleep safely in the unshakeable belief that our world will still be there, carrying on without us, with all its dramas, hustle and bustle, ready and waiting to warmly greet us in its sameness and familiarity when we awaken each morning. But do our senses betray us - is our world real or just an elaborate illusion – is it in fact, only a dream?

The other world we sometimes hear about is less familiar. The non-physical or spiritual world is only referred to in myth and legend. It is preached about on church pulpits and alluded to by astrologers and clairvoyants. It's the world we hope to go to when we die. It is known mostly as heaven, the home of our soul, our spirit – the abode of God.

Some say there is also a world called hell, where we are told we go if we are bad and sin too much. We all hope to go to the world called heaven and not hell, but either place is preferable to oblivion – to not being any more.

Even our knowledge of the world we live in is very limited. We are only familiar with the tiny little bit that surrounds us. No matter where we go, it is still only one little piece of our planet that we interact with, the rest is always only what we see or hear about in the media, or what others tell us.

In essence, we exist in both the physical and spiritual worlds. The only way we can attempt to discover our intimate relationship with both is by using our imagination. So come on a magical journey to the Two Worlds we live in.

There are two ways in which we can regard ourselves. One way is the way we usually think of ourselves, as a physical being, but although we rarely think this way, we are also a spiritual being.

Both these ways of looking at ourselves is correct for we exist concurrently in both these completely dissimilar worlds, or realms and both are relevant to us personally.

The world that we are accustomed to is of course our physical existence in the finite world of time and space. It's tangible; we can reach out and touch it. We are certain that we know who we are. We have a name, a body, individuality; we are different from them, those and others. As we look out at the world around us, we regard ourselves as different from everyone and everything out there seen or unseen that shares our space on this physical level.

On the other hand, our existence as a spiritual being in an infinite, timeless, spaceless world is less clear. There is no substantial proof - we cannot reach out and touch it - it is intangible. Our belief in our spiritual nature is simply that – a belief. We may believe a variety of scenarios as to who we are spiritually; then again, we may not believe at all. That's our prerogative.

Our spiritual beliefs were formed early in life, (from birth to around age five) consisting mainly of the second hand beliefs and opinions of others. We were given many explanations about our spirituality, we inherited our parent's beliefs that they inherited from their parents and so on, back through our ancestry.

The different religions that abound also had an input into our belief system, no matter whether we went to church or not. All of this believing what others tells us inhibits our natural ability to enquire - to search for our own spiritual roots – to find out who we truly are.

Religious beliefs that we are taught to be true are spurious at best. Our teachers gained those beliefs from old books such as the Bible, Koran and other religious manuscripts. The problem with that is that over time the human scribes, who re-wrote those ancient religious texts, added their own prejudiced viewpoints, therefore changing the meaning and the words, thus rendering them unusable as a tool to discovering who we truly are.

They may contain some truths but they are so hidden in rhetoric that it is very difficult to find. It's the same with going to church, which is okay in itself; the problem is when we believe what the preacher on the pulpit is saying, because he is getting his information from those same ancient, contaminated sources.

We are only aware of the physical half of ourselves, so how can we ever discover the truth of who we are? We must look within our own mind. Whatever we do, we mustn't believe anything from an outside source, no matter how plausible it may seem. Believing someone else's opinions or beliefs immediately stops us from ever finding out for ourselves.

Certainly listen, read and digest the meaning of what any person, religious or otherwise is trying to convey but we must allow ourselves the freedom to decide what our own truth might be, otherwise we'll become stuck in a quagmire of ignorance and continued reliance on someone else's truths, not our own.

Learning who we truly are is made a lot easier when we realize that there is something within us that already knows, so it's not so much that we need to learn anything, rather we need to remember what we already know but have temporarily forgotten.

We might say to ourselves, 'What's that got to do with me? I have no interest in anything spiritual.' This may come as a shock but we are all destined to learn (or remember) - it can be in this lifetime or it may take quite a few more lifetimes, but eventually we will fully understand who we truly are, both physically and spiritually - so why not start now?

We are spiritual beings more than we are physical beings really, so why is it so difficult for us to answer the questions about our spirituality? That's because we are attempting to find finite answers to an infinite question. Consequently, it can never be fully resolved while ever we are here on this physical level, for we are all finite beings imprisoned in this finite world.

It's no different than trying to describe a world in another dimension. It is impossible for a three dimensional being, such as we all are, existing in a three dimensional universe to describe say, a one, two, fourth or fifth dimensional world. Try it.

Attempting to describe the spiritual world, brings up the same problem, only there seems be an urgency deep within us to understand it, for we have an inner sense, a yearning, a faded memory that that is where we truly belong.

Because of our innate connection with this mysterious spiritual world, mankind has tried to understand what it is and our involvement in it from time immemorial. Philosophers, Sages, religious scholars and ecclesiastical denominations of all kinds have tried to define our spirituality, but all have failed miserably.

Some hypocrites think they know and even preach to us that they know, but they don't, they only delude themselves and us, doing more harm than good, for they too are mere mortals. As a result of their ignorance, a whole lot of miss-information has accumulated over time, burying the truth even further into the morass of superstition and belief.

The spiritual world cannot be described in earthly terms of time, space and things, because in the spiritual realm there are no 'things', therefore there is no space between any-thing, there is no past or future, so there is no time to elapse. It cannot be 'up there' or 'down there' or 'anywhere.' For that to be so, it would have to be a world in time and space, which it isn't.

It is nowhere, yet everywhere. That's the dilemma we face when trying to understand and explain the infinite spiritual world in finite terms. We need to understand something that can never be fully understood using our present mental development. We need to further heighten our conscious awareness - to advance the evolution of our mind.

Also we must remember that all this spiritual stuff is mental exercises to absorb the meaning of, not to believe. If we believe, the learning stops. As an exercise then - let's tell ourselves a story about maybe how it all began.

In the beginning, All That Is is an intelligent energy, awareness, a knowing. It has always been from the beginning which never began and never ends. It was content with itself. The spiritual realm contained only love, joy and peace, for in a world with no time or space or others, there cannot be opposites.

There is no time or space for harm or unhappiness to exist. There is only the benevolent All That Is - or God - or Universal Intelligence – God might be easiest, as long as we don't make the mistake of confusing this God with the god of religion.

God was completely content with his own company, yet had a yearning to experience and know himself, but in the spiritual realm where he was everywhere, he had no way of comparing himself to anything else, for there was no-thing else but him.

God contemplated this and realized he needed to create a world that had others - for companionship and comparison's sake. He had a dream and in that dream he created the heavens and earth - a finite, physical universe consisting of time and space that would allow the creation of others - someone over here, something else over there, not just God everywhere.

God was pleased and set about doing his creating. This took millions of years in our finite timeline, but to God, it took no time at all. God was pleased with planet Earth as the staging ground for his daring endeavour. He also wanted to create some sort of mechanism, a form that he could use as a vehicle in which to experience himself in the physical world. So he experimented and began to create the species of the earth.

Creating life on Earth began with God playing with the primordial soup - mixing into this concoction, bits of this and bits of that until finally creating a single cell creature. You can imagine God's delight as he realized that this single celled organism was the ideal building block upon which to create the perfect physical life form in which to experience his self.

Trials were carried out in the waters of earth as he thought it was the best medium for experiencing physical life. God combined more of these cells together to build more complex organisms until the earth's oceans were teaming with life. God realized however, that as the earth cooled down after the fires of creation, that maybe the surface of the land would be a better environment for him to inhabit.

So God arranged for some of his creatures to come out of the waters and inhabited the land. Firstly, God thought big was better and created the dinosaurs. After about 160 million years in our time, God came to the conclusion that maybe it was not such a good idea after all, so reluctantly he surrendered all the big cuddly fellows to extinction, as they kept stepping on and squashing his newer creations, forcing God to do it all again.

God liked the design though, so created new species based on the originals and called them reptiles and birds. The newly created ones were a lot smaller and a whole lot safer than the bigger versions, but God had decided anyway, that they were not the perfect vehicle for experiencing himself.

With the creation of souls, God had a means of testing his creations with multiple experiences. The souls, being a part of his individuality, did not actually inhabit the creatures at this stage, but hovered just above their head, experiencing their life's journey in the physical world but always retaining the knowledge of God and truth.

Although a suitable life form for God had not yet been found, at least now there was a physical environment that was well established as the staging ground for his 'Getting to know himself journey'. He had only one major creation left – finding the perfect vehicle.

Aeons would pass on earth before God was satisfied with a life form that would make the perfect vehicle in which to experience his self. The souls were now living the lives of God's many creatures, testing out each different life form for suitability, before the final design was decided upon.

This took quite awhile in earthly terms, for remember, God might be all powerful in the spiritual world but he was a bit of a novice in the physical world, for he had never done this before. One of the many creatures God created was an ape in which he was well pleased. It was not perfect for the job at hand, but was getting close.

God fiddled with the apes design, changing it here and tweaking it there and eventually a new life form was created - Man. Man was not so much a descendant of the ape but a new creation based on the idea of the ape.

When completed, the man species was considered perfect for the task. It was so perfect in fact that there have been no new species created since. As God had done with his many other creatures, he created a rudimentary intelligence that was part of the physical body, (in man it was called the ego) that was subordinate to God and the souls.

During the test runs, the souls continued to hover over each new human - just above the cranium - as they had done with the other creatures, where they experienced the life journey of the entity whilst still retaining the knowledge of God and truth. Two sexes had been created for all life forms early on, well before the creation of man, as a means to procreate. God placed the urges and impulses into each sex so as to attract them to each other.

He designed the act of copulation to be very alluring and sensual to ensure that the creatures of each type would come together so as to reproduce and populate the earth with their particularly species. God was pleased - and by crikey, so were we all. What a dull world it could have been. Yes, God was certainly a pretty smart cookie.

When the trials were successfully completed and God was happy with the human life form as the vehicle in which to experience his self, the souls entered the mind of man instead of hovering above the head. There they remained for the duration of the individual's life, while a curtain of ignorance was drawn and the souls forgot the truth of who they really were.

Unknowingly, we are those souls and only when our physical life ends, will we remember the truth. God did this on purpose, for if the souls retained the knowledge of the truth as they did in the beginning, every time they fell on hard times or their suffering became too great, they would tend to give up and return to God.

By forgetting they were eternal beings, they fully accepted their earthly body and existence as their only reality, instilling in them the instinct for survival and the fear of death. This was advantageous to God as it added depth to the experience of life's drama.

Once each soul's physical journey ended, it would remember the truth and return to God from which in reality, it had never left - for the soul is part of God's dream. When death occurs, only the physicality of the soul, the body and the ego ceases to exist.

After a respite in the spiritual world, each soul returns to the physical world, inhabiting a different human identity to continue the life experience. This 'reincarnation' occurs countless times for each soul until the soul comes to know creation in all its aspects, then it takes up permanent residence in the spiritual realm, becoming a companion of God.

We might wonder what happens to the person we think we are after the demise of the ego and body.' This perplexing question has generated a whole plethora of myths, legends and beliefs over the ages in an attempt to ease our uncertainty and stem the fear of our own mortality and threatened oblivion.

This misapprehension, perpetuated mainly by religious institutions has scared the living daylights out of all of us ever since human life began. To ease our uncertainty, we need to realize the fact that we are not who we think we are. We are our immortal soul pretending to be us.

Knowledge of the truth was blocked from the soul's awareness, which added to the believability of the life experience. God gave the souls free will however, which meant that while the soul experienced a lifetime in a body, believing it to be their true identity, they would have the ability to choose and direct their own activity without God's helping hand, allowing them to learn from their own mistakes.

The cycle of lifetimes consisted of an unlimited number of physical incarnations. Each time the soul would have the opportunity to learn more. This learning would be remembered by the soul and carried over from one life time to the next until all lessons were learned. This saved the need to learn a lesson more than once.

The choosing of the human identity that the soul would inhabit each lifetime was not random but carefully planned before the life began, depending on what the soul still needed to learn. This dictated what the human personality, looks, handicaps and attributes would be like.

Also the basic life story would be mapped out to suit the soul's agenda, a story that could be altered slightly by free will if certain lessons were learnt, plus the physical location and the ethnic group would be of importance for the life experience.

If a lesson was learned, the soul would not have to repeat it. If the lesson wasn't learned, then it would arise again in the next life and so on until learned. As the soul learned, it would advance until it came to know creation in all its aspects. Then there would be no need to return to the physical world.

The soul would then remain in the spiritual world, becoming a companion of God as was the ultimate plan. The problem we face here is that it's our ego that is trying to understand all this, but never can. It's important to remember that.

We are scared of death, of not being anymore, which is what is in store for the ego. But we are not the ego, we only think we are. In reality we are an eternal spirit experiencing a life of form. It is only the ego that ends its existence with the demise of the body.

The world we see is a hallucination, a dream. It does not exist except in the mind of God. A dream of a world of form, created by God to enable Him to get to know Himself via the soul - and as we are the soul, we are in reality God Himself experiencing that life. The ego/body is the costume we are wearing for the physical role we are playing.

Some religions, philosophies and other teachings try to convince us to be rid of the ego. They say it's a drag on our progress towards our understanding. The same goes for the body. They try to teach us to meditate, to transcend the body and ego, thus allowing us to get closer to God.

What a load of rubbish! When God created the universe and souls, the ego and body were also a part of that creation and for good reason. They needed to exist for they both play a vital role, in fact without them; God's experience of Himself would not be possible.

God's plan for the human body was to act as a vehicle for his journeys through many life experiences. The plan for the ego was to be the physical witness to that journey. We can compare the body to a limousine and the ego, its chauffeur.

The job of the chauffeur is to drive the car wherever directed by the passenger, plus keep the vehicle full of fuel, oil and water, tighten any loose nuts, (that can be a problem) and get rid of any waste material.

The soul is the passenger - directions are given by the soul to the ego via intuition. The ego is supposed to dutifully obey, but problems arose when the ego began to think for itself. It thought about the past (sometimes with fondness, sometimes with regret) and to anticipate the future (sometimes with eager expectation, sometimes with fear).

Being unaware of what was happening in the present moment because of the countless, noisy thoughts filling the ego's mind, it could not hear the intuitive instructions given by the soul and thus, lost its way. It has been lost ever since.

While ever we believe we are our ego we will live in the past and future – in memory. The present moment will remain hidden behind a disconcerting cloud of indiscriminate thought. The past and future gives our ego the illusion of individuality, of beingness. If we lived in the present moment, we would not 'be' anymore - and that's what we (as the ego) are most afraid of.

If we were brave enough to stop thinking and live in the present moment, we really would cease to exist – as the person we think we are - but we would continue to exist as a different awareness of self, an awareness that has always been there within us, but has been covered up by the thinking ego.

We would continue with our life as usual, but not as who we presently think we are and that is what our ego is most afraid of, (that is what we are afraid of) the fear that we will wake up and discover the truth of who we really are. That is why it is so difficult, for there is a part of us that doesn't want to wake up.

The ego has taken charge by thinking, thus usurping power. Our soul, believing it is now the ego, accepts this physical world of time and space as reality. The chauffeur and the passenger have morphed into one with the upstart ego now in charge. That is why we feel so forsaken by God in a world gone mad with war and strife.

Why doesn't God step in and answer our prayers? Because in the beginning, God gave the soul free will. God cannot intervene without contravening that gift. Has God then abandoned our mortal soul whilst we are here on earth, leaving us to the mercy of a tyrannical ego? No! It's exactly the opposite.

There is no need for God to intervene. The life drama is simply that - a drama – a story in which we (as God/soul) experience and learn. We find that very difficult to believe and some of us will bluntly refuse to believe, but we are only looking at it through the ego's eyes - and it doesn't want to see.

Although God would not step in and aid directly in man's progress because of his gift of free will, he supplied us with plenty of helpful advice along the way. Many ancient texts have appeared over the duration of man's existence including the Bible that was created by God as a helpful instruction manual to guide us through life.

The Bible contains many truths to aid our progress towards this end. The problem is that it has been so contaminated over time by early scribes that held personal prejudice's and vendetta's against anyone not of the same religious leanings, therefore subtlety changing the text to suit their own particular agenda and religious beliefs.

Some sections of the text was either deleted completely or changed so dramatically owing to the scribe's interference that the true message has been lost in antiquity, resulting in the Bible text being mostly clouded in myth and innuendo.

One set of instructions given to mankind by God was the Ten Commandments, which outwardly seem to be authentic moral instructions. But how many of those commandments were changed surreptitiously in some way by the self serving ancient scribes?

The first four commandments could well have been purposely added or altered in an attempt to force the population into submitting to the scribe's bigoted and narrow religious beliefs. 'You shall have no other God but me' – 'You shall not make any graven images' – 'You shall not take the Lord God's name in vain' – 'Remember the Sabbath and keep it holy'.

In other words, do as they command or else my angry God will not be pleased. The remaining six make good sense: 'Honour your Mum and Dad' – 'Don't kill' – 'Don't commit adultery' – 'Don't steal' – 'Don't bear false witness' – and – 'Don't covet your neighbour's wife'. All are common sense guidelines for an upstanding life.

We are not threatened with the wrath of a vengeful God if we do other than what they command; instead the responsibility for following them and the consequences if we don't falls directly on our own shoulders, regardless of what our religious beliefs might be.

Another important set of instructions given to man was 'The Seven Deadly Sins'. These directions were harder for the scribes to distort into suiting their own prejudicial agendas, so they carry a lot more truth than the commandments. All of these seven warnings hold true today, regardless of one's religious beliefs. If we commit any of them, it could indeed prove to be deadly - to our quality of life anyway.

Let's go through them and their opposites:

> *Pride*- Opposing virtue- Humility.
> *Avarice/Greed*- Opposing virtue- Generosity.
> *Envy*- Opposing virtue- Kindness.
> *Wrath/Anger*- Opposing virtue- Calmness.
> *Lust*- Opposing virtue- Chastity.
> *Gluttony*- Opposing virtue- Sharing.
> *Sloth*- Opposing virtue- Zeal.

It's simple. If we commit one of those seven sins, we suffer, regardless of what we believe, if we have the opposing virtue, we will live an upstanding life, again, regardless of our beliefs.

The most deadly sin of all for mankind in the present day and age is *Avarice/Greed*. Have a think about it.

Big companies like the banks and our governments are all consumed by greed. All are self-serving for the want of material acquisitions. Amassing great piles of paper and metal that man has deemed to be worth something, with no consideration or compassion for the human element.

As long as they can make a killing money-wise, they simply don't care if people suffer because of their selfishness. The second most deadly of these sins in today's world is Pride. 'My religion is the only true religion.' Your beliefs- whatever they are - if different from mine make you idiot, an infidel or a terrorist. Believe in what I believe or I might consider killing you.

The current wars in the Middle East and elsewhere are either fuelled by religious bigotry or a greed for oil. (Another way of accumulating those pieces of metal and paper we call money) These have been the two main reasons that have sparked the anarchy in most of man's ridiculous and senseless wars. Included in this anarchy is the genocide being committed in some African countries at the moment as well as the past, where the greed of the arrogant few is for despotic dominance!

Long ago, God sent man a set of written guidelines to follow, (from many sources, not just the Bible) for a successful and inspiring life. The problem is that mankind has not fully heeded those wise words, therefore is suffering the consequences.

God's ultimate plan for the soul, which is of great importance in our understanding, is that when God created the cosmos and souls, the cosmos that he was referring to was the entire universe, which not only includes Earth and our solar system, but also the rest of the Milky Way Galaxy and all the other galaxies in the known and unknown universe.

The physical life journey of the souls was to be experienced in many places in the cosmos, not just on Earth. To imagine for a moment, as we used to in years gone by that Earth is so special as to be the only planet to harbor life is as naive as believing that the Earth is flat. Today, most of us realize that even though science has still not discovered any proof of life other than on Earth, they eventually will.

We as souls, live many lives in many places in the universe. In God's dream, the souls were to have a series of incarnations, (physical life experiences in a number of bodies) until they had experienced every aspect of human life.

In other words, in all our many lives, (and our soul remembers every one) we accumulate knowledge and learn all the necessary lessons until we have no need to return to Earth. There is no time limit, no penalty for not learning, no judgment day, no purgatory where we are held until a vindictive God decides whether we are worthy of heaven or hell.

When the soul was as free in the physical body as out of it - then the cycle of earthly life would be finished and the soul could go on to new adventures. We have lived in many bodies and have known ourselves by many names, learning more in each incarnation. This we will continue to do until we have no need to return to Earth again – but our learning experience will carry on - in other places in the cosmos.

Although God had granted the souls free will, so would not directly intervene in their learning experience, He did provide helpful guidance in written form, plus would occasionally deem it necessary to send a soul directly to the physical world to help mankind, a soul that had completed the experience of creation and had returned to God to become a companion and co-creator.

The soul is known to man as Christ. This Christ, as with this God should not be confused with the Christ of religious doctrine. The Christ soul (recognized by us today as Jesus, although there were many others that preceded him) was interested in the plight of his brother souls, so took human form from time to time, to act as a leader.

In the early stages, the Christ soul occasionally 'took on flesh' returning to the physical world to teach and lead mankind. These incarnations were neither born nor died, but only appeared when necessary. To aid mankind further and give guidance in later times, God found it necessary to have Christ born of woman, as a new individual, a new soul record, so as to be fully accepted by mankind as 'one of them', though behind this new individuality shone the pure light of the Christ soul.

It was necessary that the knowledge of truth be hidden from the mind of this new individual, so he could be as one with the common people. A veil of ignorance was thus drawn on the awareness of his true self while the underlying Christ soul could begin his pilgrimage to help mankind.

The last Christ soul incarnated was Jesus as far as we know, and he as Jesus, led by example; eventually triumphing over death and the physical body and became the way for man to follow. Although it may seem that our prayers are not being answered, God is sending us continuous help; we don't need to be religious or go to church, we only need to be still and become aware.

Nothing that happens to us happens by accident - *Ever*. Every event, every tiny incident, whether seemingly good or seemingly bad has a purpose. Everything is there for a reason including what we see, read and hear. Whatever is needed will appear magically in our life when we are ready to receive it - not before. We are the ones who put all of this together.

Every part of our present life and all our previous lives were predetermined by us before we embarked on this present lifetime. We can vary our journey slightly as we go by virtue of free will if it allows more learning but all in all our life's journey follows a predestined path.

That path is towards enlightenment. To remembering who we really are. We are the cause of it all - no one else - for in reality there isn't anyone else. We exist in one world while dreaming of living in another. The spiritual world comprises only love, which is something we can't comprehend here in on Earth.

As magnificent as a world like that would be to us, comparisons are impossible. Appreciation of a perfect world cannot be fully experienced unless there is a contrasting opposite to compare it with, which is why we are here.

Contrasting opposites are experienced in time, which is an illusion of the physical world. It is part of the same dream, so can change pace depending on what our soul requires. The illusion of time can be proven in our own life experience, for example, when we are young, time is not slow or fast - it simply doesn't exist.

Each day is enjoyed to its fullest by most children without fear of time ending the fun. It starts to interfere with our life when we go to school, especially with such ordeals as exam studies. It gets to be very noticeable during our adult working life. If we toil all day in a dreary job, endured for the sake of money, time between start and finish will drag on and on.

Then it flies by during the evening until our work day begins all over again. Although our work week takes forever to go by, the weekends and holidays pass by like a flash and then before we know it, we're back in the grind again.

In later years, time passes by at an ever increasing pace. One day is quickly replaced by another. All of a sudden there doesn't appear to be enough time to do anything before it is nightfall and time once again for bed. As the wrinkles grow and the aches and pains increase, more time is spent in reminiscing than living.

The lucky ones who really enjoy life to the full, do not suffer this time warp nearly as much, in fact it remains similar to what it was in childhood. Each day is full of enjoyment and satisfaction no matter what they are doing. But there are not many of us who are experiencing such a life at this stage of our development.

The physical world is made up of separate things. The prerequisites are three dimensions, time and space, matter and thought. They are all co-dependent in the making of each other. Each plays both an integral and complimentary part in a world where there must be, by necessity, others (two or more objects interacting together).

Each is a separate entity which, being a material object, must have a certain height, width and breadth (three dimensions) which distinguish it from others. This enables opposites to exist both physically and mentally that can be compared to one another, hence, experience and learning become possible.

These objects whether living, inanimate or mental, have a space between them and it takes time to traverse that space, even though that time may be minuscule. It even takes time to travel between atoms. Without time there could not be space and vice-versa - without a space between objects, time could not exist.

The same holds true for mental objects. There is a space between thoughts. In the physical world, because of time, all objects are finite - they have a beginning and an end. They exist for a time then they don't exist, whether the objects are animal, mineral or mental. The only difference is the length of time between being and not being.

That is the fundamental difference between the physical world and the spiritual world. In the spiritual world time does not exist, therefore nothing can have a beginning or an end. Also, because there is no time, there cannot be any space because time and space are inextricably linked together.

With there being no time and space in the spiritual world, experience of a self (compared to another) is impossible. That is precisely the reason for Creation. The creation of the physical world enables experience of self - which includes learning about self and others through trial and error.

In the spiritual world, the only way to experience a self of any kind is to dream of a world in which this is made possible. That dream is the three dimensional physical world that we experience in our human lives.

It must be remembered that it is all a hallucination. It is a drama played out on a make-believe stage of matter, time and space.

Thought gives the illusion of time. In reality everything is happening now, in the present moment. All experience and learning is accomplished now. God's ultimate plan is unfolding now, not yesterday, not tomorrow but now. In the spiritual world - in the absence of time - there is only now. The reason for our sense of time changing so much depending on our activity and age is our ego.

Time and the ego are both part and parcel of the dream of a physical world. Neither of them is real. The ego lives in time - the remembered past, the anticipated future. This is accomplished by thinking - in fact, the ego does not exist out of time or thought.

The ego cannot exist in the present moment, where there is no thought. That is why it is so hard to stop thinking. The ego does not want that, for it means its end, its death, and because we are under the delusion that we are our ego, we are fearful of our own death if we stop thinking.

When we go to the cinema, we usually decide beforehand what we would like to see, a movie that is maybe filled with lots of drama, romance or plenty of laughs. It could be scary, horrifying or one of suspense and human survival, depending on our choice. We then sit back comfortably in our seat with our popcorn and ice-cream and enjoy the show. We may cry tears of joy or sadness, recoil in terror, or even roll about the aisle in hysterical laughter depending on the movie genre but we are always aware that it is only make believe. It's just a movie.

Unknowingly the exact same circumstances apply in our physical life experience. It is filled with all those same emotions that make us laugh, cry, love, hate, scream, shout, etc. The only difference is, we are unaware that it is just fantasy, a dream, make believe. Our 'life movie' is no different than the movie in a theatre, except that it appears more realistic. Imagine for a moment that while watching a movie, we believed it was real, forgetting for the time that we have a normal everyday life outside the theatre.

When we walk back out into the light after the show is over, we would suddenly realize it was just make believe. With a sigh of relief we'd then exclaim

Wow! Everything's really okay. That wouldn't happen though would it? We are not that silly!

The 'you' that believes this world is real, is our ego. It is part and parcel of our body and the physical world. To the ego, this world is real, this is all there is. When our body comes to the end of the road, so does our ego. This world ends and so does its existence.

Our ego can never know of the spiritual world. It can never visit, stay or settle, or even take a peak, it is out of bounds. But that is not the case for our true self - our soul. We have temporarily forgotten who we really are, believing instead we are our ego, so as we can sit back and enjoy the thrill of suspense, drama, romance and comedy in our own life movie.

Before we take on a new physical life experience, we/our soul, chooses the script, for want of a better word that will make up the story for the life movie we wish to experience. The script contains the lessons with their positive/negative contrasts our soul needs to learn on our journey towards full conscious awareness. But at the same time, physical life was meant to be enjoyable - unless we take it all too seriously of course.

Before our incarnation, we know the physical world and the human life form we are about to enter is only a dream, but we want to become fully involved so as to experience all aspects of that particular life journey, so during, or shortly after physical birth, we purposely forget who we truly are, believing for the duration of the life term that we are this fictitious ego with a body and a name.

This enables us to fully immerse ourselves in the physical drama. Once our life term comes to an end, we re-enter the light and remember the truth of who you really are - eternal and indestructible. Experiencing physical life whilst believing we are this ego with a body and name has caused us some problems however.

We tend to take it all too seriously, suffering negativities like anger, anxiety, frustration and the fear that we will suffer either physically or mentally, or that our very existence may be jeopardized at any time. So then, how can we possibly relax and enjoy our life movie?

Not by any physical or mental effort, that is only our ego trying to do what is impossible for it to do. We need to stop trying to control our life, instead have the courage to trust in the process, become aware of the now moment and unconditionally accept whatever is happening in our life, without trying to change it – for the truth is, we can't.

We must stop thinking so much. We should try to just enjoy the movie. We are someone entirely different to who we think we are. We will remember the truth when our present 'life movie' ends and we return to the light. Then, with a sigh of relief we'll exclaim "Wow, why was I so anxious? Everything is really okay"…

Realizing that the world we see is an illusion, a world that's created to provide the lessons we need to learn, is very important for our progress. Once we understand that, we tend not to take life quite so seriously. If we relate it to watching a movie, we are then able to stand aside somewhat and view it without identifying with the ongoing life drama. More like a spectator or bystander.

We always have the choice of changing movies if what we are seeing is not what we want. We can get up at any time and go to another theatre. Of course we also have that opportunity by committing suicide, as too many people do, but that is not a solution. Another unsatisfactory way to avoid facing the world and its necessary lessons is by over dosing on drugs.

Why? Because, once we leave our physical body and the physical world, we return home to the spiritual world. The curtain of ignorance is lifted from our mind and we remember everything, including why we chose that particular 'life movie' in the first place. We chose it prior to incarnating so as to learn the lessons that it held.

To take our own life on purpose is to leave our 'life movie' before the lessons are learned. It's quite possible some of us have done this in many prior incarnations. If we have, each time we returned home to the spiritual world, we would have said to ourselves "Damn, why did I make that same mistake again." Remember, the lessons are repeated until learned!

Our voluntary choice then would be to re-incarnate into a similar 'life movie' where those exact same lessons, that we needed and wanted to learn, would once again be presented to us. If we cop out again, it will be repeated again and again, life after life until we learn what we need and want to learn.

We are doing all this ourselves, no one else. There is no angry God up there waiting to judge us or a devil down there waiting to stick a pitch fork into us. There's only our self - It is our curriculum - We have made it all up.

Fulfilling God's ultimate plan requires us to learn the lessons presented in each lifetime before we can proceed onto the next. There is no blame metered out if we fail to learn. When we were a child in kindergarten and we could not recite the alphabet correctly, we did not chastise ourselves, and we certainly didn't leave class because it was all too hard.

We worked on understanding our ABC's until we became proficient at it. Once learned, it would never have to be learned again. We could then tackle other subjects in our curriculum. It is important to realize that while here in the physical world, we could regard ourselves as children learning the lessons of life from scratch.

We are allowed to make mistakes. There are no penalties except those self imposed. We are a much loved child of the universe. So, suiciding, drug overdosing or any other means of avoiding life's problems purposely brought upon ourselves is not the answer. Then what is? What do we need to do to progress?

Learn the lessons that life gives us. Lessons such as Compassion for our fellow man and all of earth's creatures - Love and respect - Kindness – Understanding – Care – Forgiveness of others as well as us - Generosity etc. - Something inside of us knows them all.

When the going gets tough, change your life movie if necessary, move away from a place of violence or suffering if you are sick and tired of it, don't turn to drastic measures like suicide or drugs. Realize that it's all happening for a purpose. Remember that whatever our situation, it is there to teach us something and if we look hard enough we'll see that it's not as bad as it first seems.

We want and need to learn, that's an agreement we made with ourselves before we came here. One great thing about this physical world though is that there is a thing called time. Time passes and what is maybe quite painful and traumatic now is soon relegated to the past. If a lesson is learned, it is learned forever, so go ahead and learn to be a loving human being.

There is a mantra in 'A Course In Miracles' that reads: "I am willing to exchange the world I now see for a world that I can love and understand." This world is still an illusion, the same as the one we now see, but if we seriously want the world we see and experience to change for the better, some earnest inner work on ourselves is needed before we can achieve that aim.

Each one of us must be willing to learn to be honest, responsible and compassionate, within our heart, not outwardly for some kind of reward, before our world will change. Sounds like very old fashioned values and that is exactly what it is.

Can you imagine for a moment, a murderer murdering someone if he holds these values in his heart, or a rapist raping, a thief thieving, a bully bullying? Can you imagine an angry person or a jealous person venting their negative emotions on some poor innocent victim if their inherent nature is peaceful and loving?

Can you imagine there ever being a war between people and nations if the qualities of love and understanding were instilled in mankind? And can you imagine there ever being poverty in the world if we all cared for each other, showing loving compassion and generosity toward all our fellow human beings?

Of course not! It would be a completely different world than the world we now see. And that world begins within us. We must be willing to give up the world we now see before we can accept a world we can love and understand. The world we now see is there for a purpose, for us to learn from, but it's time for change, it's time that we moved on.

The warning signs to look out for are greed, selfishness, pride, envy, lust, anger, jealousy, any form of violence; we know them all; The Seven Deadly Sins and all that. We must become consciously aware of what we are doing to this world.

We must learn to be loving and caring human beings. That is our ultimate goal. That is exactly what we are doing here – and it's up to each one of us to succeed.

Fundamentally, we are unaware of our true nature. When we sleep, we believe our dream-self and dream-world is real. When we wake up, our dream-world gives way to the waking state and we recognize that the dream-self and dream-world are actually empty of substance. It's quite easy for us to realize that they are only fabrications and projections of the mind.

In contrast, as we go about our normal daily life, we perceive the world to be made up of solid and separate objects. We believe that our thoughts and the objects around us are real. But, could it be that even while awake, our thoughts and objects are also fabrications of the mind, as empty of substance as our dream-self and dream-world?

Usually we have no reason to question the validity of these beliefs, but there is every good reason why we should. All dream and waking phenomena; thoughts, emotions, sensations, images, and the world around us, are constantly changing. Everything about our body, mind, and the world is constantly morphing from one thing into another, a mass of swirling, changing sensations, emotions, thoughts, and images.

We want life to be consistent and predictable, so we suffer, because life around us is constantly changing. Our habitual self is forever searching within this sea of instability for something stable and constant to hold on to, while the inner fabric of each of one of us is deep calmness and peace that is stable and steady, and is recognized to be ever present even in the midst of life's tumultuousness.

This is what is referred to as our essential true nature, our innermost self. A deep peace that we know without a shadow of a doubt is always present. When we inquire into the who, what, and where of the awareness that is witnessing life's changing phenomena, we discover that this "I" that we take ourselves to be is not solid either and paradoxically, unlike everything else, isn't changing.

We realize that our True Self, or true "I" ness, is an infinite, spacious presence of being in which everything, both waking and dream states is born, unfolds, and dissolves. We discover the truth of our True Self, as Pure Being.

No human being at our level of understanding or below has ever left indisputable proof of what happens before birth or after death. It's all conjecture. A person who has reached that stage of understanding while still alive has by consequence moved further up the pathway of enlightenment and is no longer within our field of awareness, we simply would not be aware of their existence.

Therefore everyone in the world that we are aware of is on the same level of understanding as us, or a bit below, so no one is capable of telling us the truth. All theories are just speculation. The very worst thing we can do is to believe what others believe - and yet, that is what millions of us do.

Our body and personality are created at birth and the death of our body means the death of our personality, (the person we think we are). Neither our body nor our personality can return to this world, it's a one way street despite stories to the contrary.

To fully remember, a soul must have passed from the physical level to the spiritual level, leaving the finite body and personality (ego) behind. Once there, the soul would have no wish or need to return to the physical world just to let us know what happens.

Nobody at our level has any idea of what the truth might be. All the books that we may have read by prominent scholars, whether religious or philosophical cannot tell us the answers. They can only give us pointers towards the truth - and sometimes, away from the truth.

Everyone must remember the truth for themselves. If a philosopher or a religious zealot states in their teachings or temples that they know the truth and to believe and follow them, they are either thoroughly deluded or making it all up for a purpose which is usually greed or self aggrandizement.

That includes all church doctrine, no matter what faith. Books such as the Bible hold marvellous insights that are there to help us learn about ourselves and assist us along the path to enlightenment, but they are not to be believed. They are meant only to be pointers towards the truth.

Comparing the physical world to watching a movie is one way of trying to understand how life works. Another way is to liken life to driving a car. We use our car to get about in. The car's computer and gauges will make us aware when the vehicle needs servicing or something's amiss. We also use our body as a vehicle to get from one life experience to another in the physical world.

It operates in much the same manner as our car. It has a computer (brain) which tells us when it needs nourishment like food or liquid and if something's amiss, our body will let us know something's wrong.

When driving our car, what do you think would happen if our mind and the vehicle mentally merged and we believed it was more than just a machine to get around in? What if we believed our car was who we were? Men in white coats would come along, kindly put us in a long sleeved jacket and take us away to a big building with barred windows wouldn't they?

It sounds ludicrous, but that is how we have come to regard our body, yet it is the same as our car, it has no life of its own. Without us there to guide it, it would be just as inert as our unmanned car, but because our mind has become confused, we wrongly believe we are this body which we use to get from place to place.

The mind is where our consciousness dwells whilst travelling around in this earthly body. This is the place where we experience and learn about our true self in form - where we get to know who we really are. This has nothing to do with the normal, physical functioning of our brain which houses the body's computer.

When our life adventure is over, we step out of our human vehicle. The body becomes unusable because it has no driver (us) and as with an old or wrecked car, eventually decays and returns to the earth from whence it came. Who is this '*US*' then that guides the vehicle called the human body? It is our eternal, spiritual self. That is who we really are.

Remember the Pixar movie "Cars"? The star of the movie was a little red car named 'Lightning McQueen' and his sidekick was a tow truck named 'Mater'. In the movie there was no driver behind the wheel of these cars and yet they were portrayed on the screen as being intelligent - cars that had separate personalities and were aware that they existed as individuals.

Now what if that scenario was true to life? Just imagine if it was reality and cars were curious enough to experiment on other cars and themselves to try and find out how they operated. What made them - them. What made their horn toot! They would lift the bonnet and take apart the head, the block, remove the pistons, etc.

They would learn all about themselves, how they ran, what role each mechanical part played in their mobility and sustainability. They would learn to be able to do repairs, to fix and replace faulty parts that broke down or wore out, to lengthen the life span of all cars, no matter what model, make or colour.

They would also learn why they needed a constant supply of fuel, oil and water. All that stuff that is essential for their survival but, they would be at a loss to find any evidence of their self awareness - their identity - their individuality. How they knew that they knew.

They would be unable to find their *'IS-ness'* by pulling apart a car body because it is not there. The driver is undetectable behind the wheel - as the movie depicts. It is the same with us human beings.

Our driver is invisible and undetectable. It is not a part of the physical contraption we use to get about in. We can dissect and examine the human body all we like but we won't find what drives us.

Like a car, our bodies are only a vehicle to get around in - they have a use-by date. They will eventually break down, wear out and be discarded – but we will not. As with our old car, we will simply dispose of it and get a new body to replace the old – next lifetime.

Imagine for a moment that a soul is having a dream of being a human body with a name and history, living in the drama of a three dimensional world. In reality, the whole physical world including the human body and everyone and everything else in it, is within that soul as the dream it really is.

For the duration of our physical life our soul does not realize this, believing the dream as being reality. Compare that scenario by imagining going to bed tonight and having a dream. The dream seems real and appears to be occurring outside of us. When we wake up in the morning, we realize that the dream was inside of us all the time and not reality.

Because we have experienced this many times in our life, we take it for granted. Then take it for granted that when we wake up tomorrow morning from our night's dream in the physical world - we are still dreaming - and will continue to do so until our task here is completed…

As one diamond has many individual facets, we are all individual facets of the one God. This enables the one God to experience multiple lives. It's important to realize that whilst we are the one God, the different facets (souls) are experiencing a smorgasbord of separate lives. Being a facet of the one God, we remain an integral part of everyone and everything else in this world – and everyone and everything else is an integral part of us.

Thus we cannot hurt, harm or damage any other living creature without hurting, harming or damaging our self, for in reality, they are all us. At the opposite end of the spectrum, we cannot love and appreciate any other living creature without loving and appreciating ourselves - and receive love and appreciation in return.

We are worthy of every bit of that love and appreciation whether we realize it or not – and so is everyone else. If we are part of everything else in this world, how then do we only experience this unique personality that we think we are and not be aware of the rest of the living creatures that we are a part of?

Imagine for a moment, the confusion if all life experiences were clumped into one. The maelstrom of sights, sounds and senses would render any learning experience or enjoyment impossible. Life experiences must be separated and that is precisely what the ego is for. The ego plays a vital role - in fact, without it, the experience of life in the physical world would not be possible.

Multiple life experiences are gathered from all the separate facets of the one Soul Awareness via the ego and once we make our transition back to the spiritual world, we will then have all of those experiences at our disposal. The individuated ego (the person we

Mind WorX

think we are), will then have done its job and will cease to be, as will the body.

This causes great fear in us only because we think we are our ego/body and that when we die, we will be no more, but we do not die. We cannot die. Only material things in a material time/space world, such as egos and bodies can die – but we are not of this world.

Energy, which is what we are in essence, can neither be created nor destroyed. All of the energy in existence has always been present in the universe created by God. Time and space are one illusory fabric of that universe; you cannot have one without the other. This is the basic premise of modern physics. But in reality there is no time therefore there cannot be any space.

Without time and space there can be no separation or individuality. Energy cannot be separated, it is one entity, a positive force with no boundaries, which cannot be broken up or divided in any way. This is the eternal and ubiquitous root of the universe. The illusion of time: A weekend of enjoyment passes by in the wink of an eye, whereas a twenty minute wait for a shop to open takes forever.

Word need time and space. All physical and mental activities in a three dimensional universe are reliant on there being a space between objects whether material or mental, a space that takes time to traverse or elapse. For instance, there is a space between the words in this sentence and it takes time to read or hear that set of words.

In a universe other than three dimensions, say a one or two, or four or five, there would be a completely different set of laws. These universes would behave in ways that would be impossible for us three dimensional beings to comprehend – and so would a world with no dimensions at all - such as the spiritual realm.

And yet, a part of us does understand the spiritual world very well. Our nonphysical self is very comfortable in this world, for it is our true and familiar home where we belong - a world that in reality, we have never left – except in our dreams.

So how do we communicate in the spiritual world? There is no need. Why? There is no 'We' - there is only One. There is no one else. There can't be anyone else. For that to be possible the spiritual world would need to have dimensions, time and space, that would allow separation and individuality like the physical world, but it hasn't.

It is infinite. It has no boundaries or restrictions. Within it our soul is omnipresent; we are everywhere. There is not a place where we are not, for there is not another place to be. We have no need to communicate with our self. We are Universal Spirit - We are God – who has forgotten the truth temporarily while we are dreaming of being here, inhabiting a physical body in this world.

While we are experiencing physical life, words are necessary to enable us to communicate, understand and survive in our environment. We also need a body and a human mind for an individual, conscious experience of life.

These are all essential, finite components of this physical world that allows us to communicate with others while experiencing ourselves in three dimensional time and space. Even when we are contemplating spiritual matters, we are handicapped by our need to use words in thoughts or on paper.

We exist in both the physical and the spiritual worlds simultaneously. The physical world is easy for us to understand. It is tangible, we can reach out and touch it, feel it, smell it, hear it, see it - It is made of matter and appears to be very real. The spiritual world on the other hand, is harder to understand. It is not touchable or see-able or feel-able by our physical senses.

It can only be believed in - or not believed in as the case may be. Most believers call it Heaven, Nirvana, Utopia or some other exotic name - some even call it Hell. Also, its location is believed to be either up there, down there or out there somewhere. In reality it is not up there, down there, out there or anywhere. It is no-where – yet everywhere.

To be in any one location at all it would have to consist of time and space – but it doesn't. The spiritual world is time-less, space-less, dimension-less; therefore to us three dimensional physical beings, it is understandable-less.

The reason we can't comprehend the spiritual world no *matter* how hard we try, is that there is no *matter* in the spiritual world. It is completely foreign to our understanding while we inhabit a body of *matter*, think with a mind of *matter* and live in a world of *matter*, in a universe of *matter*.

The spiritual world does not follow our laws, it is everywhere around us. It is not composed of time or space or matter. It is our eternal home where we are right now in the stillness of the present moment, creating a dream that enables us to enjoy many physical lifetimes of drama, comedy, sadness and happiness on a small spinning ball of rocky matter we named Earth…

❞You are learning to appreciate who you truly are, by experiencing the contrasts of who you truly are not.❞

CREATION

FROM the first moment we poked our inquisitive noses out of our caves and gazed transfixed at the breathtaking vista that lay before us we were the creators of our world – albeit unconsciously. Being novices we were incapable of consciously creating anything with any degree of success, therefore The Creator was at the helm of the ship of life, guiding us and keeping us on course.

We firstly needed to learn how to survive, ensuring the continuation of ourselves as a species. We also needed to learn how to compassionately co-exist with others before we could be trusted to take a turn at the wheel of life and become competent, conscious co-creators.

Obstacles were placed along our course to add challenges as we experienced and learned, slowly becoming more proficient and more trustworthy, for we had been gifted with the highest intelligence of all Earth's creatures, entrusting us with the position of caretaker of the planet and everything in it. Our aim was to eventually pass muster and consciously steer our own course.

Imagine for a moment what this world would be like if mankind was let loose with full conscious control of his own creation today. With our complete disregard for others and our environment; what a right mess we would make of it. We only need to look at the destruction and mayhem we are causing now, whilst our creating is still being done unconsciously.

Without a guiding hand at the helm, our selfishness, greed, anger and senseless slaughtering of our own kind and other living creatures would only risk our own extinction, taking with us, many of the other species if not the whole world with us. We can easily understand The Creators caution and reasoning that we need some mental maturity first.

That is the only reason we are not conscious creators now. We are still novices learning the ropes. There is nothing wrong with that, for that is simply the level of evolution we are at today, but now the time is fast approaching for us to fulfil our destiny and play a leading role in God's Creation.

Conscious awareness of our true identity reveals the fact that we are eternal spiritual beings having a physical adventure, thus our human existence (in one form or another) is forever assured. Our course has been indelibly charted on the ship of life towards an ever unfolding destiny full of excitement and positive challenges. There is an intelligent purpose to Creation.

It is essential for us to be here for we are God in physical form. With awareness of our true reality we will have the ability to consciously co-create the next exciting era in our ever unfolding physical voyage. This is the challenge we are being given right now - and it is up each one of us to accept it and do our part.

The ship of life is causing a wake that draws us along and even though we may stray off course at times, the wake irresistibly draws us back towards the ship and eventually, as we learn to master life, will allow us to climb aboard and consciously assist in steering our own course as well as that of all life on our home planet.

As more of us learn, the wake becomes stronger, drawing evermore people behind it and when we realize that there is no need to struggle against the current, but to simply trust and allow the forward momentum to carry us along, the easier it will be and the faster we will approach our destiny.

Until then, while our soul is wide awake and enjoying the journey, we are asleep and missing out on the fun of Creation, for the ship of life is carrying on regardless. For us to take a turn at the helm, thus making a conscious contribution to the joy of Creation, we must wake up from our spiritual slumber.

It is up to each one of us to have the trust and allow the current to draw us forward, attracting others to follow us as we go, (the one lighted candle effect) eventually bringing everyone on board. Once we are there, it is not then the end of Creation, but just the beginning of the next exciting chapter in our physical journey.

The blueprint for Creation is an infinite plan that as a consequence is timeless, so it never began and will never end, but because our physical nature demands both a beginning and end for us to comprehend something that is in reality timeless, we have to pick an imaginary starting point. There are two main assumptions as to how the universe came into being:

Theology: Whose estimates are based on a literal interpretation of the Bible calculates a time span that varies from around 6,000 years plus or minus 2,000 years for both the age of the Earth and the rest of the universe.

Science: Hypothesizes that the universe began with a 'Big Bang' between 12 and 16 billion years ago and the forming of the Solar System, including Earth, at around 4.8 billion years ago.

We still require some sort of an ending, some point in the future when none of this will be anymore. This is more spurious and again we look to both science and theology for some sort of explanation for an impending Armageddon that would be acceptable to our human understanding of things. But no matter which way we look at something that is in reality timeless, we can never fully comprehend it.

In the physical world that we inhabit everything that is new eventually becomes old and dies, decays, rots, rusts or perishes. We can only begin to understand timelessness when we have awakened to our true reality. Once we are awake our whole understanding of life is re-aligned. We still experience time while we are here, but we also have the inner knowledge of the timeless reality that is our true nature.

With that understanding we don't take this world of time and space too seriously anymore and it becomes impossible to fear death for we know that we are eternal. We are not separate from the process of Creation; we are part and parcel of the whole shebang. We are all unconsciously contributing to where we are going in every moment of our stay here.

Once we awaken to our true reality and begin to consciously contribute to our journey through physical life, what experiences will we then create? What exciting adventures are in store for us then?

The choices we make, the actions we take, what we say, what we don't say, are all adding to the momentum of this vast cosmic unfolding of Creation – an unfolding that we are creating as we go. What we do impacts on the whole. There is no end to physical life, it is an ongoing experience. As we create new ideas, more ideas crop up, more challenges are created for us to solve. That's what Creation is all about.

As we become more consciously aware, one habit that we need to break is the tendency to speak about the world as if it exists 'out there.' We cannot separate ourselves from the process of Creation, because when we do we fall into a false or dualistic way of thinking.

Because we are unconscious in a spiritual sense, we tend to look out there for solutions and apportion blame onto others when our problems are not solved. Nothing is 'out there.' It is all 'in there.' We have to look within our own mind for the answers, for that is where the answers lay. Each one of us is on an inner journey of discovery.

This is a journey that we all take collectively and yet it is at the same time, a very personal experience. That is because we are all connected. What we each experience affects the experience of others and humanity as a whole. We are many in body but one in spirit.

We must be consistently on guard, impartially watching our every move, not only of what we do, but also what we say, feel, think, assume, judge and believe. To look 'out there' for the answers is to be looking in the wrong direction. That has been our biggest handicap against becoming conscious creators up until now.

When we really embrace the truth that we are not separate from the process that created us, but are in fact contributors, (even though we contribute unconsciously at the moment) then we need to become very clear about all the ways in which we are actually affecting the process, so that we can begin to consciously take part in a more positive and evolutionary way.

Once we become consciously aware of the wonderful adventure we are on, we will then truly understand both ourselves and our environment. Then in our awakened state of being, our prospects become limitless. We will have the whole cosmos in which to create, conquer and explore in our search of adventure and knowledge.

Earth will eventually become overcrowded, which is a problem that we will need to address. In certain scientific circles, some naysayers are of the opinion that overpopulation threatens the mass extinction of our species and possibly the destruction of our planet, but in reality that is not the case. It is but one of the many challengers that has been purposely set before us to tackle and conquer.

Explorations of our nearby neighbours, the Moon, Mars and eventually the other planets in the Solar System will allow us to set up places of future habitation for humankind as well as other species that share our planet. As physical time progresses and Mankind becomes more experienced, we will venture further out of the solar system into the greater cosmos to colonize other star systems as our own Sun nears the end of its life.

Setting up places of future habitation will be crucial. Meanwhile at home, science and technology will need to continue conquering sickness and disease. Mother Nature's natural disasters will still devastate our world, but all these problems are an intentional part of the blueprint of life that will continue to provide us with the necessary challenges we need to face and solve while on the leading edge of physical experience.

It must be realized that this is all physical evolution. It has nothing to do with our spiritual evolution.

Our soul is simply enjoying the physical learning experience through our body's eyes and emotions. All is coming to pass as intended as part of our ongoing physical journey. The only problem is that as yet we are unaware of the significance of it all.

If we remain unconscious of what is evolving, we will keep meddling in a process that in our unconscious state we are incapable of handling. Just as important, while we are getting ourselves unnecessarily in the way, we are missing out on the fun and glory of Creation.

Buried deep in our subconscious is the knowledge of the truth of Creation, but because it remains dormant within our psyche, a fanciful narrative was fabricated in the collective subconscious of man to attempt to explain how the universe came to be. One version of this story is in the first book of the Bible - Genesis.

Being passed down to us through many scribes and orators from antiquity, over time it became a mixture of misinterpretations, innuendo and personal prejudices. The story of Genesis tells us that God created the universe and all that it contains in just six days. This revelation infers that God is a physical being living in a world of time and space like us.

God does not exist in time or space at all, His existence is timeless and spaceless, so although six days may seem to us a very short time to create a universe, whilst scientific theory suggests a more reasonable time span of between 12 and 16 billion years, in reality, God Created the universe in no time at all, for time did not begin until after Creation.

God is not a physical being. There is *no body* called God, there is only Intelligent Awareness, an energy that is everywhere and yet nowhere at the same moment. We can get an inkling of that intelligent awareness by becoming mindful of the awareness behind our eyes.

That intelligent spark of awareness is what we identify with as being us, but where exactly is this intelligence? Can it be touched? Is it within our brain, if so whereabouts in our brain, or is it maybe behind our eyes, or is it somewhere else?' Despite much advancement in the study of the human anatomy, science has never been able to pinpoint where it is.

God's Awareness is exactly the same as our awareness - it is in no particular place, it just is. The only difference between us and God is we appear to be wrapped in a physical body and live in a physical world. God is not wrapped in a physical body, nor does not live in the physical world as such - but He does experience the fruits of His Creation - through us.

Stripped of our physicality and three dimensionality, (form) leaving only the awareness of self that sits behind our eyes, are we really God in essence? In other words is the self awareness behind our eyes, God experiencing our life journey?

Admittedly whilst we are housed in our human body in this three dimensional world, we are handicapped somewhat by our ego's intellect, (the person we think we are) making it difficult to distinguish between our God or Soul awareness and our habitual thinking mind, for both reside behind our eyes.

If we could stop thinking just for a moment, thus losing our individuality so to speak, would we be able to more clearly see who we truly are, which then brings to mind the possibility that if we could further strip away our individuality, (identity) would we then also realize that the awareness behind our eyes is God experiencing not only our life journey, but the life journey of each and every one of us?

There is an old saying, 'You can't see the forest for the trees'. In relation to what we are discussing here, metaphorically speaking, are the trees that are blocking our view, 'Physicality' 'Three Dimensionality' and 'Individuality' (form and identity) and if we could see passed those obstructions, would we get a glimpse of the truth?

Not to say we should discount, ignore or get rid of these three obstructions, for they are an intrinsic part of our spiritual forest and thus meant to be there. But because we are so close to them, are they blocking us from seeing the whole picture? Do we need to learn to step back from ourselves?

Without our physicality, three dimensionality and individuality, we and God would be one and the same, wouldn't we? We would all be the one Creator, the One Intelligent Awareness experiencing and participating in the whole process of Creation.

If all of that were true, we would in truth be God the Creator, the one that created the physical universe and all the things in it in the first place? Somewhere deep down in our soul, is there a residue of memory of the beginning of the universe - and our participation in Creating it?

Insinuating that we are God may seem a bit presumptuous – but only to our ego's habitual sense of self that is caught up in an emotional whirlpool of unworthiness and self doubt. Because of this, we, or more precisely, the person we think we are, does not believe for one moment that we would ever be worthy of being called God - and that is true, we are not, but who we think we are is not who we truly are.

Once stripped of our form and identity we would all be God. Is it possible that there really has only ever been The One Intelligent Awareness experiencing physical life through each and every one of us? Is there a residual memory of our Oneness as The Creator hidden deep within us, and would that memory also have been in the minds of the scribes who wrote the Bible's story of Genesis?

Was that their subconscious inspiration for recording it? Seeing that time did not begin until after Creation, why then did they choose six days, a really short time to create a universe we would all agree?

Their residual memory would have been faded and sketchy at best and they were physical beings to boot, restricted to living and thinking in a world of time and space, so it would be natural for them to pick some sort of a time limit for Creation otherwise the story would not have made any sense?

Also, because of their latent spirituality, to them, the story of Genesis would have been an esoteric, out of this world event – like is depicted in our present day science fiction stories. Did they choose six days to fit in with the mystical, super natural quality of the story of Creation?

Being like us, creatures of form and identity, (the obstructions to seeing the truth) the scribes wrote down the story using the written word, the only way in which their physical minds could interpret any meaning and credibility in such a magnificent and overwhelming event such as how the universe began.

Attempting to understand how the universe was created is like trying to understand a two or four dimensional world. We three dimensional beings could not possibly imagine such a world and trying to comprehend how the universe was created in no time at all is even more difficult. We can only conjecture, for whilst we inhabit this world of time and space we will never know.

We are stuck here in a physical body in a physical world of time and space whether we like it or not. Our problem is we think we know everything, if we can't understand something or it doesn't fit within the physical boundaries of our limited understanding, we class it as bunkum, or gullibly follow a theory based on what someone else believes rather than using our own mind.

Genesis' story of Creation is a mythical story of our beginnings. It was never meant to be taken literally, regardless of what some religious zealots may say. It has also been adulterated over time by later scribes of certain faiths, who altered and added to the original text for spurious purposes in the hope maybe, of aggrandising their particular religion above all others as the only one true faith.

So when describing the Creation of the universe, those scribes who were honestly trying to remember what was hidden deep with their minds could have written a time span of six days or six years or six billion years, it would have made no difference. The time taken could never have been settled, for the universe is in truth, ageless, something we cannot understand.

Both science and religion's determinations for the age of the universe are as plausible as one another, for in reality the universe has no beginning or end, so physical time does not really come into the equation at all.

That residual memory of Creation is within us all. Underneath our habitual ego mind there is something else there, a quiet Intelligent Awareness that knows the truth of who we really are. An Awareness that knows that we are God, that we are The Timeless Creator of every-thing, we just don't realize it yet.

Suggesting that within our physical persona, we really are the One Creator in multiple forms brings about a further startling question concerning the Creation of the universe. Could there truly be anyone else here? Could there ever be anything separate from this One Self?

If we go way back to before the beginning, before thought, before feeling, before our body and mind, before the world and the whole universe was created, what would be there? There would be only you wouldn't there? - You are everything.

The question is, does the universe really exist, or is it just a dream of this One Self - and if we were stripped of our Physicality, Three Dimensionality and Individuality (form and identity), would we be this One Self - The Dreamer? When we dream of a night, do those dreams contain a time element, or is time irrelevant?

In your dreams, do you think you could create your own universe? If so, how long would it take? Would you need to stay dreaming for a few billion years or so or could you not only create your own universe during the length of one dream, but relax and enjoy your Creation afterwards… And by the way, how long is one dream anyway?

Would you be free to experience the wonders of your Creation in subsequent dreams, adding new features here and there as you learn and experience, subtracting the bits that you find unsuitable? Just imagine the fantastic universe a Super Mind like God could create in a dream - well you don't have to imagine - you only have to look around you. Are we that Super Mind?

Our ordinary nightly dreams feel realistic but the truth is they all occur within our mind as we realize each time we awaken. Are we only dreaming of the world that is around us out there, during one of our regular spiritual sleeps? When our present life experience is over, do we cease to be, or do we simply wake up like we do here from our earthly dreams and continue on to our next Creation?

Mankind is at a distinct disadvantage when it comes to understanding the story of Creation. We are restricted to using our ego's everyday mind, so when we view anything, it must come from a physical perspective. In other words, it must consist of a physical form that's enveloped in three dimensional space and be reliant on the passage of time, or it doesn't make any sense.

God can only be imagined in these physical terms, as an old bearded man dressed in a white cloak say. But that is not true. God is not physical, God is Spirit, Divine Intelligence, the very Essence of us all – and that is a revelation we can never comprehend whilst we are wrapped up in our physical cocoon of a human body.

The same problem arises when trying to understand Jesus Christ. Jesus was an ordinary man, born in Bethlehem, lived and worked in Nazareth and died in Jerusalem. He was no different than any one of us, subject to similar emotions, likes and dislikes etc. But he was also Christ; Christ was his spiritual self, his soul, his eternal essence.

The only difference between Jesus and any other man was that his 'Christ' mind was more developed – for we all have a 'Christ' mind within us (soul). At the end of his life, it was Jesus the man who died and was placed in the tomb; it was Christ his spirit that survived death, not Jesus the human body.

The same mindset comes into play when we are told we are the Creator of our world, we can only regard ourselves in physical terms, and as humans, we did not create the universe at all- our human body and persona was *Created* with the rest of the universe.

Our human attempts at Creation would be impossible, but it was not our humanness, it was our Beingness that created the universe, our spiritual essence, soul, our Inner Christ.

We are human beings. When we die, our humanness ceases to be, but our Beingness continues on for eternity. God, Christ, Being, Spirit, Soul - We are One with All of That.

"Your true eternal existence is so overwhelming and sacred, that in comparison, your mundane human life is inconsequential."

THE LIBRARY

IN EVERY town and city, in every nation in the world, there are libraries. They hold within them the complete recorded history of man, his environment and the history of the universe as man knows and understands it. Within the mind of man there is also a library, one that is far more expansive and complex than any library out there.

Our inner library is within each and every one of our minds. The librarian is the ego, the person we *think* we are. It records each and every moment of our life as memories, automatically storing them away for safe keeping, like librarians do in the libraries of the world.

Both the inner and outer libraries can only record events of the past, once they have happened and become a part of history, even though some of those events may only have occurred a fraction of a moment before in time, it is still a part of the past.

As our personal records (memories) and the records kept in our physical libraries get older, they are less used, so as time goes by, they are progressively relocated further and further back into the libraries dark recesses.

Within each of our personal libraries, the records are held of all the memories of every single event, every taste, every smell, every feel, every sight, every sound and every emotional reaction to every event we have ever experienced since the day we were born, whether we judged them good, bad or otherwise.

As the recorded memories get older, they are harder or sometimes impossible for us to recall, but the ego remembers them all and uses them constantly as a ready reference to enable it to decide how to respond to any new event that occurs in our life, based on the memories of what it did in similar situations in the past, for anything new is a potential threat to the ego's continuing survival.

Collectively, the libraries of the world hold within them all the information concerning the history of man and his environment from when history was first recorded to the present day, including his many discoveries, achievements and advancements in the sciences, which includes his explorations and deliberations of the land, the planet and the universe in which he lives.

Likewise, within the mind of man, beginning at the time of his first appearance on earth, the collective ego has been accumulating a far more complex library detailing the inner mental workings of man. What his beliefs, judgments, prejudices, ideologies, idiosyncrasies and the manner in which he collectively thinks about his world are.

When anything new takes place in the world, our reaction to it together as human beings is based on the collective ego's records of the past – what we did last time. Because of this, we do not see nor recognize, therefore do not react to any new event for what it is, fresh, vibrant and dynamic, but look at it through the dirty lens of the past – instantly correlating the new event with that which is already known.

By way of the mind's collective ego, our world leaders organize and run our governments, corporations, institutions and societies by referencing and generally following what was done in the past. In this way the collective ego makes and imposes laws and regulations that control the lives and actions of the populace, based on those records stored away in the collective ego's voluminous mental library.

Again, anything new is a potential threat to the survival of the ego, for if we should *ever, ever* awaken from our spiritual slumber and realize the fact that we can happily live and prosper in the present moment, without relying on what happened in the past to organize and run our lives, the ego would become redundant.

The ego does not want this of course, for it would mean it's demise, so it's responses and reactions to every new event, passed on to us and the leaders of our nations via our collective subconscious, is always based on the old, the stale, and especially the safe and known past.

Outside of our ego's library is outside of our mind. We have never been 'out of our mind' and as long as we believe we are our ego, the person we think we are, we will never take that momentous, life changing step. Why? Because, being outside of our mind everything is new, fresh and dynamic and very, very scary, because it is unknown.

We have nothing to reference it against. There are no records for newness. When faced with the unknown, we are made vulnerable. We falsely believe that newness will hurt us somehow, or maybe we won't even exist 'out there' anymore. Anything could happen to us and we wouldn't be prepared to protect ourselves.

We cannot defend ourselves against something we don't know and understand and we can never know or understand anything that is new. Newness is something that has never happened before obviously, so we would feel very unsafe and insecure.

It's like as if the librarian at our local library believed that reality existed only within the walls of the library and nothing existed outside of it. No matter how many times we tell her not to be silly, that there is a wonderful, exciting world out there just waiting for her to explore, she hasn't got the courage to step outside.

While she has access to all those old books about what happened in the past, she feels safe and secure. If something does occur that she doesn't quite understand, she is not worried for she has her trusty reference library close at hand.

By categorizing the new event, she can then file it under similar, known events of the past that she does understand, or even if a little unusual, she can make it fit so it conforms to what she already knows.

We are the same as that librarian, imprisoned within the walls of our own mind, believing we are the incessant thinker between our ears, misinterpreting the outside world through eyes dimly. While we live our lives that way we will remain too fearful to ever risk the newness of living in the present moment.

Harking back to our librarian, should she ever dare venture outside of her library, she would find herself in a very strange place, a place where she has never been before. No longer having access to her trusted reference books of the past, she would feel very vulnerable, exposed and in danger.

If our local librarian really was like this, we would explain to her that with a little bit of courage she would find that the outside world is a safe and exciting place to be. Taking her hand we would then gently coax her to remain outside in the light, but she would recoil in terror, rushing madly back inside to the safety of her books of the past.

That sounds like a rather insane scenario but that's exactly how the majority of us live our daily lives. The ego is our mental librarian and, believing we are the ego, we confine ourselves to our mind's dark interior where everything is familiar, safe and known.

Our ego, like our body, has a use-bye date. At some time or other, we all must experience our own physical death, no matter how much we eat healthy and exercise, no matter how much of a fortune we accrue or how many life insurance policies we hold, our ego, with our body will cease to be - and this thought terrifies the ego.

People who have near death experiences often comment that at the point of death their whole lifetime flashes before their eyes – every living memory, every event, every high, every low and every emotion, passes in front of their eyes in fast motion.

What is happening as their physical death approaches is their ego is being dragged forward from its lair at the back of the library, passing by the records that hold the complete memories of their lifetime from birth onwards as it is convulsed forwards towards the light outside the library.

For those people who have returned from near death experiences to tell their tale, their ego has been strong enough to overcome those forces, and freeing itself, has scampered back into the depths of the library and the safety of the past.

Eventually our ego must succumb to the ravages of time and although we may be kicking and screaming all the way to the threshold, we must finally face the light outside – which for our ego means death and oblivion – but not to our true selves. In truth we have experienced the end of many, many lifetimes and so physical death holds no threat to our continuation.

For our ego though, death has never been experienced before. Death is the newest of the new - and the most feared, for it does not survive - and it knows it. This might appear callous, but a person who fears change or newness in ordinary day to day life is destined to experience a rather traumatic ego death, for their ego's extrication from the safe and known confines of its mental library could be quite a terrifying experience.

Depending on our ego's resistance, the duration of our journey to death's door will vary. The story goes that on the other side, all our loved ones that have transitioned before us will be lovingly waiting to give us a hand to help rid us of our illusion of the ego and hence it's needless terror.

Maybe that is the 'soul' purpose of their attendance at this time, so our transition will not be so frightful, but come what may, eventually our ego will dissolve back into the nothingness from whence it came, revealing to us once again who we really are and always have been, reunifying us as our true eternal non physical self.

When man was first created, he was given a memory. It was an essential component for the survival of the human species. Without it our race would have become extinct within a very short time. To help man survive in a then alien world, he needed to remember what happened in the past, both to him personally and to the species as a whole.

He needed to remember such things as what animals were dangerous and what were good to eat, what plants were nutritious and what were poisonous. He also needed to remember how to protect himself from the elements, how to light a fire to keep warm and how to stay cool when he got hot etc - etc.

In man's early evolution, this learning phase of trial and error cost the lives of many of his own kind who were unlucky enough to make the wrong choices, but because of their sacrifice and mans ability to remember, he learned from their mistakes, ensuring that the race of man as a whole, thrived.

This ability to remember is still essential for us today for we need to remember our language and how to communicate, we need to remember our name and the names of family and friends, where we live and countless other mundane everyday tasks that help us survive and function as a physical human being in a sometimes harsh and indifferent environment.

That's what our mental library was originally created for. Our memory of the past was to be a ready reference to help us get through the day as a physical human being, we were meant to subconsciously scan the records ourselves when we needed to remember how to perform a certain task during our normal daily routine.

There was no one in charge of this memory bank, no librarian, apart from us ensuring our own physical wellbeing, we were meant to spend the greater part of our human life experience, living in and fully experiencing the vibrant now moment.

Remembering the past was originally meant as a tool for survival, then later as an aid to ease the everyday running of a physical life, but sometime during man's early evolution, this ability to remember seemed to acquire a mind of its own - an entity that we now call the ego. The ego does not really exist; rather it's more of a mental disorder.

In reality it is our soul, or true self that has become absorbed and deluded by the past, resulting in us believing that we are this constant thinker in our head, this ego self that inhabits the now but lives in the past.

We can prove this if we really wanted to, we need only have the courage to stop thinking and become fully aware of the now, but could we be that brave? If we stopped thinking of the past, we would have no ego and while believing we are the ego that would be a very difficult thing to do, for we would mistakenly believe it would mean the death of our self.

It won't be, in fact it would be our liberation from a lifetime of tyranny, but we can't find that out without taking that first step and once taken, there is no way back, we can't change our mind half way. We can't ever know for sure what will happen for we have never taken such a step before, and this *'not knowing for sure'* causes all our fears and keeps us imprisoned in our deluded state of mind.

Walking out of our mental library and leaving our past behind means exactly the same as enlightenment, conscious awareness or awakening that spiritualists and philosophers write about. Once we are out of our thinking mind, the illusion of the ego is gone forever, but surprisingly, we will still be there, the library of our past then falls back to its original purpose as a ready reference put at our disposal.

We then resume doing what we were meant to do, experience what it's like to be a human being and we do this best by living in the vibrant and ever renewing present moment.

What exactly does it mean to step out of the mental library and leave our past behind? It may sound a confusing and rather inane thing to try and do. But if that was the case, why is it made out to be such an important step in our personal growth, and why would taking that step be so hard for us to do?

Walking out of our library of the past means leaving *'our self'* behind, or more precisely, the self we think we are, a self that we have grown very fond of and attached to since birth. Our mental library holds the story of us, who we have been over the course of our lifetime that, as the thinker between our ears, we continually tell ourselves in our mind.

This includes all of our wishful thinking about ourselves, what we want and don't want and those very private thoughts that we keep to our self and would not dare tell another living soul about.

All are memories of who we once were, so when we think or talk about our self, we are really referring to the person we once were in the past, not to who we are now – and that includes our imagined future, which is only old memories of who we once were projected forward.

If we did let go of the past, we wouldn't be able to take any of those memories with us, we wouldn't be able to think or talk about our self at all for there would be no old us to think or talk about anymore.

Although being fearful of losing our identity if we did take that step, our body and name would go with us, but the difficulty is, we won't be able to take our past with us, we must leave that behind.

Outside of our library - or we could say 'outside of our habitual thinking mind' – there is only the ever renewing present moment – and that would be terrifying for our ego self. Why? Because our ego self can never actually go there, for it would mean its end.

Connected to our soul/true self, the ego is an integral component for our complete physical experience. It is our body's intelligence whose only purpose is to look after the running of the human machine, but somewhere along the line it overstepped its boundaries and took over our sense of identity.

It is this mistaken sense of self that is causing all of our problems. To end the illusion, we need to stop *'thinking'* that we are this false ego self that's in charge of our body's maintenance not our life, and reconnect with who we truly are. To do this we must step away from our past and move into the present.

Once we do that, we will find that the world is born anew every moment. For example, when we look at a rose or a sunset, there will no longer be any old memories of either roses or sunsets to compare them with. They'll have a freshness and vibrancy all of their own and in the instant we drink in their fleeting beauty it will be gone, to be replaced in the next moment by a new vision.

It is the same with every person we meet, whether loved ones or people we don't like. Outside of the library, there will no longer be any memories of what they were like last year, yesterday or even a second ago, there will no longer be any stale baggage from the past. We will accept them unconditionally, just as they are in the now moment - and accept them once again in the next moment and the next - and the next.

Now, how hard do you think it would be to leave your past life behind? Pretty hard AY! - But not to our true self. Our true self is already like that, and always has been. So to change our life experience from the pain of the false to the joy of the truth, all we need do is change our sense of identity from the past to the present.

The only reason it's so difficult for us to leave our past behind and live in the present moment is that we believe we are this constantly thinking chatterbox in our head, and while ever we have this false sense of identity, that's the last thing in the world we would want to do, for it would mean the end of our illusory self – the ego.

Understanding this academically is not good enough, for any mental effort we use would only be ego effort, and the ego will hoodwink us if it can by pretending to be a sincere seeker. 'Oh Yes!' we (as the ego self) proudly exclaims, 'I now understand what it's all about and I am now fully awakened and living in the present moment.

We may think that we could happily live with that, but what about the pain? Our ego would continue to be what it always has been, selfish, greedy, cruel and uncaring and if we don't toe the line we will be punished, as we are now, with anxiety, depression, unhappiness, anger, despair. We would not be free at all but would continue to be at the mercy of our ego self.

In the meantime, our soul/true self continues to do exactly what we came here to do, experience a human lifetime. Having the courage to step out of our library of the past will allow us to 'catch up' so to speak and consciously join in with our true self, in this exciting journey.

Leaving our library of the past and living in the now would not mean that we would suddenly cease to be our ego and become our soul - rather with self awareness; we will shed our delusion of the ego, leaving it to look after our body, while we reunite with our soul - a unity that we have never really lost.

Our soul has one purpose for being here and that's to experience a physical lifetime. It is curious; it wants to know what being a human is all about. So it is repeatedly born into this world, each time attaching itself to a physical body, to explore experience and learn.

Whilst our soul does this, our library of the past is used as a ready reference to remember the dos and don'ts of past experience. This helps the ego, the body's intelligence, to run and maintain the mundane daily tasks of living and surviving in a material world.

Our soul has specific missions it uses to help give our lifetime a focus. These missions could be to learn what was not learned in previous lifetimes, or to learn something as yet unexperienced, or it could be to teach, where our soul learns to help other souls complete their life plans.

We all have an agenda that our soul decided on before attaching itself to our body. They're narrow enough to give life a certain composition, yet broad enough to avoid limiting our free will, thus allowing flexibility as we progress.

Beyond its specific missions for each lifetime, our soul is seeking something much bigger. The grand purpose if you like, is to unite with our physical self

- allowing us to become consciously aware during a physical lifetime that our soul awareness and our physical self awareness are one and the same.

In our souls learning experience, it is not just positive feelings it is after, it wants to be entitled to them. In our eternal home there are no negatives, only positives, so while living in a material world, our soul learns how to appreciate them.

Our soul does this during a human lifetime by contrasting the positive experiences against the negatives. By experiencing the pain, sorrow, loss, unhappiness etc of physical life and overcoming them, our soul can then feel entitled to and thus appreciate the good things, both in our physical lives and also later, in our spiritual life.

Using the physical body and its five senses, our soul has the ability to fully experience the emotional melodrama of human life, for apart from our mental library holding the memories of the past that are needed to negotiate our way through the hazardous maze of daily life, it also contains the memories of all the emotions we have ever experienced.

These are used for contrast between opposites (good, bad, positive, negative) and as we learn over lifetimes, conscious awareness of our true purpose grows and expands. As an increasing number of us connect with our soul/true self, it will become easier for others to follow. (A rising tide lifts all boats, as the saying goes.)

Yet strangely, despite our soul's mission to fully experience the human condition, both good and bad, while we continue to identify with our ego, we are constantly searching for shortcuts to feeling good and avoiding the ones that we deem bad. Thinking that we (our ego self) knows best, we have invented myriad quick fixes to try and avoid the ordinariness of life – like the use of drugs, alcohol, chocolate, over eating, sexual addiction, extreme sports, etc.

Not to say that any of these are bad in and of themselves but we need to become consciously aware that we may very well be using them to get away from the humdrum of ordinary life - which in reality is not to achieve happiness, peace, joy or any of those things – but to experience pleasure.

To try and stop using a shortcut without understanding our egos need for it, only makes the situation worse, for there is always a cost involved after experiencing a high brought on by a quick fix. The price we pay as a result is dependency, cravings, addictions - and the pain of their accompanying withdrawal symptoms.

The belief that we can rely on shortcuts to happiness, joy, rapture, comfort, ecstasy etc, rather than earn those feelings leads to legions of people who in the middle of great wealth, fame, business acumen etc - are spiritually destitute. Positive emotions experienced without the contrasting experience of negative emotions leads to emptiness and in-authenticity.

Conversely, positive feelings that arise from the exercise of learning what is right through the experience of what is wrong and then instinctively doing what is right is authentic learning.

If we continue to obstinately stick with shortcuts, the situation only worsens over time, preventing us from advancing, and if that be the case, at the end of this lifetime's course, we will have missed an opportunity to progress, obligating us to repeat the same suffering next lifetime until we do learn. (Karma)

That is not cruel by any means, for it is our own soul that is the one who will decide on that specific course of action if it is warranted so that our physical self can learn and eventually rid itself of the egos influence and re-unite with the soul.

The old saying, 'There but for the Grace of God go I' has special meaning here, for we have all either experienced lives like the shortcutters in previous incarnations, or worse, those lessons in life are yet to come.

Our soul is eager to learn the whole gamut of human experience in one life or another. Remember that we (the separate person we think we are) are unnecessarily suffering here not our soul. If we can learn to discard the illusion of the false and embrace reality, the pain will stop.

So the next time you are criticizing a drunk, drug addict, sex fiend, shopaholic, gormandizer or such like, stop for a moment and realize that you were once in their shoes, or God forbid, you still have those shoes to wear.

The library of the past is an essential component for our total life experience. It appears though that we have misused what was meant to be an aid to maintaining the viability of our physical form and allowed it to take over our identity. In reality this is not the case, for there is a purpose to everything, but whilst believing we are our ego self we can never understand this truth.

Identifying with the ego is similar to being cast in a stage play where we wear a costume to play a role in a drama but strangely, in our life drama, once we have donned our human costume, we believe we really are the character we are portraying.

If we did not identify with the ego (which is the next stage of mans evolution) our life experience would remain similar in that we would still be playing the same role in the same drama, but we would be consciously aware of who we really are – a soul wearing a costume, playing a part in a life drama.

When we no longer identify with our ego we will then become what might be called, a freed personality, unencumbered by a false sense of self – in other words a self that is fully aware that it is temporarily housed in a body with a name whilst being fully involved in the role of a human being.

Once we have evolved to that stage, we will be much more stable and receptive to being led down more advanced avenues of learning towards our soul's ultimate aim of spiritual/physical unity. It is up to each one of us, how long this takes.

When we discard the human costume at the end of our life's drama, we will no longer be our physical self - but our awareness of self, or soul awareness - will continue to exist as we reawaken from the dream of physical life, remembering who we truly are.

Looking at it from our very limited human perspective, you could say that ninety percent of our soul remains on the spiritual level leaving just ten percent to inhabit our human body, so even though that ten percent may not remember its true origins, the other ninety percent does.

In this way, our soul can guide us along a predetermined but flexible life path using intuition (that quiet voice within) to complete the missions our soul has come here to perform. All that we really need do is stop thinking so much and listen to that inner voice.

In reality, our soul remains wholly on the spiritual level for there is nowhere else to go. The ten percent that is experiencing the melodrama of physical life within our mind is only our soul having a dream where it plays the imaginary role of a physical being living a lifetime in a physical universe.

Our identification with the ego has been necessary for without it there would have been a gap in the learning curve of our physical journey, for if we were to suddenly remember who we truly are without first fully experiencing the human condition, it just would not have made any sense, therefore our soul has purposely made us forget our true origins.

Doing this makes the human adventure much more intense and worthwhile, allowing us to experience and learn from the rigors of living in a seemingly hostile world. In this way, we learn to appreciate the love, joy and peace that permeate our eternal home.

As our human species approaches the next step in our evolution, spiritual/physical unity, the library of the past will continue to serve us well, albeit behind the scenes, doing what it was originally meant to do, ensure that our physical bodies have the best chance of surviving in a physical world.

Mankind is approaching the verge of evolving past the necessity for ego identification and once we have achieved that milestone, we will advance onward to the stage where we will have earned the privilege of consciously sharing our life's journey with our soul/true self. What a wonderful life adventure is in store for us then.

❞ You are writing the story of your life and everyone else is playing the part you have assigned to them. ❞

VIRTUAL REALITY

EVERY ONE of us experiences our own separate version of life viewed from inside what might be described in physical terms as an invisible bubble that completely surrounds us. Onto the inside screen of this bubble, we project a world we perceive to be real. It is not real; it is an imaginary world our mind has made up, depending on what we believe is real.

Each of us experiences a different world unique to us, depending on what it is we need to learn – for some, the world is calm, loving and friendly, for others it is a world of heartache, sickness and pain. For yet others it is overridden with crime, war and violence. For the majority of us though, it's a blend of all of these positives and negative aspects of life.

In reality there is no world at all, there is only the One Awareness and nothing else – and the only way the One Awareness can experience a world at all is to dream. We are that Awareness, we are that Dreamer. The dream of the world we see in our bubble or PSPR, 'Personal Sphere of Perceived Reality' is an illusion – more elaborate than our normal nocturnal dreams maybe, but otherwise no different.

While we are dreaming our nightly dreams, we believe them to be real. It is not until we wake up in the morning that we suddenly become aware of how unreal they were. It is the same with our dream of life. While we are living in the world that surrounds us it appears real, but when we die, we wake up and realize it was also just a dream.

Because we are three dimensional, physical beings, we are restricted to using a dualistic framework of words and concepts to try and understand, therefore, any explanation of the way the One Awareness experiences the multitudinous dream of physical life falls far short of any adequate description.

Even though we must use such a framework, it is not stopping us from reading between the words and concepts and feel for the truth by telling ourselves a fictitious story of one Soul's journey through a human lifetime. Before we can begin our story, we need to set the scene:

Mind WorX

Compare the bubble that surrounds us to a flight simulator used to train airline pilots. It is a windowless pod that sits on a bunch of hydraulic rams usually in an airport hangar. It is a stationary object comprising a fully fitted out flight deck. Once the trainee is inside, his sense of reality changes. The sights, sounds and movements of an aircraft taxiing to takeoff, flying and landing are simulated via surround sound speakers, front and side computer monitors and hydraulic rams outside that tilt the pod this way and that, giving the illusion of movement.

Everything inside and outside of the cockpit appears to be real but it is not, it is only a simulation of reality allowing the trainee pilot to acquire the necessary skills to fly an aircraft through all types of conditions. He also has to handle mechanical failures and other unexpected problems while experiencing the virtual reality of flying a plane, albeit safely, as he never really leaves the ground.

We are just like the trainee pilot inside his simulator except we are in a bubble that is invisible to the physical eye and senses; a 'Personal Sphere of Perceived Reality' if you will, or PSPR for short.

There, we, or in this story, the Soul who is training to be a human, is learning how to live a physical life.

Apart from operating the PSPR under normal, calm conditions, the trainee human must also learn how to handle the whole gamut of negativities such as violence, pain, sadness, as well as unforseen failures from minor to major physical malfunctions. The more time he spends in simulators the better he will be at handling any event that human life might throw at him – And so the story begins:

* * *

TRAINEE human being, Sol, nervously approached the human body simulator – better known on the Spiritual Plane as the PSPR – (Personal Sphere of Perceived Reality) that was sitting unattended in one ethereal corner of The Creator's Realm after being reprogrammed in readiness for Sol's next simulation.

Training required Sol to learn every aspect of human life. He had already mastered the basic survival techniques from many previous life simulations and was well on his way towards learning to overcome the more difficult intricacies of human emotions, like anger and fear, pain and heartache, greed and selfishness.

Sol anxiously wiped away beads of perspiration from his spiritual brow, for no matter how many simulations he had performed over eternity, each and every time there was that same inner feeling of excited anticipation.

From experience, Sol knew that while he was piloting the PSPR, he would forget who he really was so he could more fully experience the contrasts between the negative forces (unavailable on the Spiritual Plane) and the positive forces that were pre-programmed into the simulation of human life. Before takeoff, this always made him feel just a little uneasy.

The PSPR had been purposely assigned to Sol as it was programmed with the full agenda for the missions he was to accomplish this lifetime, plus the genetic code for the human that was to be his physical persona, put together from all his prior learning achievements, which was also added to the records for mankind's overall progress. Also included was the assistance he was to give other souls during his simulation, to help them complete their particular life missions, while they in turn would assist him.

He had began his training aeons ago in PSPRs much more primitive than this one where he learned the basics of keeping the human body alive. As he piloted the many simulators through countless lifetimes that included injury, sickness, pain and death, he became more proficient at keeping the simulation going for longer and longer.

The PSPRs themselves also evolved as The Creator shared Sol's and the other trainees experiences while they learned to handle human life, thus enabling The Creator to regularly update the simulators with the latest technology.

Assisting Sol in the cockpit of the simulator, (called the 'Mind') is an Instructor who sits in the co-pilots seat while remaining constantly connected to The Creator. He quietly observes Sol's progress and gives advice when needed, although no matter how many simulations Sol has carried out, he still finds it difficult most times to hear or heed that advice.

Easier to hear is the PSPR life engineer who sits in the jump seat behind Sol. He is a veritable chatterbox that never shuts up named Egor. His task is to keep records of every event, no matter how trivial that occurs during the simulated lifetime, storing them away in the computer's memory banks.

Unlike Sol, Egor can never leave the PSPR as he is an integral part of the mechanism itself. This tends to piss Egor off for he would absolutely love to visit the Spiritual Plane and indeed be like Sol, eternal. He looks lovingly at the exit every time Sol leaves the 'Mind' but no matter how hard he tries; he is unable to cross the threshold.

The truth is something Egor refuses to accept and that is, when this simulated lifetime is over, he becomes redundant. After each life simulation, all PSPR's are reconfigured in readiness for the next training assignment; both the current Egor and the memories of past events are deleted. The simulator is then re-formatted and another fresh Egor installed.

Only Sol and The Creator, retain the complete memories of the physical persona used for the present life simulation (who in reality is Sol, whilst he is what is called on the Spiritual Plane, 'Unknowing'). As well, Sol remembers all the other physical personas, the lifetimes he has experienced since the beginning of his training.

Overseeing the whole operation is The Creator whose idea it was in the first place - to create a living physical universe of form - better known on the Spiritual Plane as 'The Dream'. The Creator is more affectionately known amongst the souls as Yahweh, coined not long after 'The Dream' began and the PSPR had completed its initial trials for human survival capabilities.

Companion souls, especially those of his close family group, were also there to help Sol, whether they were involved in a simulation or not. That might appear implausible until realized that time and space are only illusions of the Physical Plane, therefore souls can be participating in a human life simulation while at the same time remain available for assistance to others when needed.

Sol settled back comfortably in the simulator and began to go through his pre-life check list as it was nearing time for takeoff - referred to on the Spiritual

Plane as 'Birthoff'. Excitement was abuzz for no matter how many 'Birthoffs' there were, every new human simulation was always an important event.

The PSPR was now primed and ready for the beginning of a new human life experience. Sol was in position at the front of the 'Mind' although he had no need to be there, for the simulator had been set to automatic when it was first fired up and the countdown to 'Birthoff' initiated, but Sol was diligent and liked to do the final checks himself to make sure all was well.

Being a part of the PSPR's computer software, Egor was in standby mode. He would not be logged on until there was enough past information uploaded into memory to give him the data necessary to function. Until then, he was quietly dormant.

The Instructor, referred to as the Quiet Observer, didn't enter the mind until Sol had the simulation well under way and Egor was fully involved in his duties of recording past data. That was when the Observer's guidance was needed for Egor's chattering interference escalated significantly as the simulation progressed.

Egor tended to think he knew better than Sol, so would incessantly give unsolicited advice. It would not be so bad if he knew what he was talking about, but he didn't have a clue, so the Quiet Observer needed to be there to try and inspire Sol to listen to him and not to Egor. That at times was very difficult for when Sol became 'Unknowing' he tended to listen to Egor rather than the quiet voice within.

Birthoff was initiated through another PSPR piloted by a soul who had been experiencing human life for quite some time and had the ability to look after the new simulation until sufficient data had been accrued in the computer memory banks to enable the new, simulated human life form to become self sufficient.

Sol needed the experienced soul's help after birthoff as well, for he had to relearn how to handle a PSPR as once settled down at his station in the newly activated 'Mind' he would become 'Unknowing' and no longer remember who he truly was or that he had guided many previous simulations.

Suddenly the parent PSPR began to convulse and contract, propelling Sol's simulator towards birthoff. Sol waited tentatively as the PSPR entered the final launch sequence. The front monitors showed a brilliant light ahead.

To Sol, the transition to the Physical Plane was uncomfortable after so long in the subdued light of the 'Un-birthed Mind' and scary too, for he was beginning to forget the truth of who he really was and become identified only with the simulated human body.

The final checks had been done and communication established between Sol and the 'Mother' soul in the birthing PSPR. All was ready - He was now at his most nervous. Yahweh tried to reassure him, telling Sol to trust in Him, but at such times, Sol usually didn't listen. Then with a rush, Sol's PSPR emerged into the bright light of the Physical Plane. Human life had begun.

Sol did not immediately forget who he really was, although his memory was fading fast. The simulator was still on automatic and Egor remained dormant, but checks had to be made and Sol was the only one who could do it.

He was already hooked up to the surround sound system and the monitors, but now he was also attached to other sensors that simulated physical life such as touch, smell, taste etc - and emotions – Sol did not look forward to them, for human emotions were the hardest for a soul to come to terms with.

Egor was beginning to rouse as the computer stored past information at a rapid rate, ensuring the human's survival - and Egor was very eager to survive. At this stage he wasn't too much of a problem, but as he became more fully operational - that's when all hell would break loose - literally. Negative emotions, those were the ones that Egor relished, for with them he could wield his false authority.

Sol was not looking forward to that, but Egor's overbearingness was to come later. Egor remained happy though, for he was slowly gaining control of the human self as Sol slipped in and out of forgetfulness. He would continue to do this for quite a while as the infant human mind slowly stabilized and became more individualistic.

The computer, sensing Sol's readiness to begin, releasing control, switched to manual and Sol began the slow integration into the role of a human being. *"Bloody negative emotions"* - It would be a long and arduous life experience for Sol - compared to the loving, peaceful joy of the Spiritual Plane that is.

It had always fascinated Sol as he mistily remembered his true source. He had been an airline pilot in one of his previous human life simulations and he likened this sensation to the flight simulator that he had once spent so much time in whilst training to be a pilot.

When he looked out through the PSPR monitors, instead of an aircraft nose, he saw an out of focus human nose. When he looked to the sides, instead of wings he saw human arms and hands, down below he saw a human torso rather than an aircraft fuselage and instead of landing gear there were human legs and feet.

Everything appeared to be so real and yet, like the view through the aircraft flight simulator monitors, they were all an illusion - made more realistic by the fact that he could also feel the human body. Sol was beginning to believe he was really a human being.

Each human being's life has an agenda of lessons and events that need to be experienced, arranged by its soul before life begins, that once has been fulfilled, will eventually come to an end in what is known on the Physical Plane as death. Although the human form with its accompanying ego awareness ceases to be, the soul does not.

It transitions with all that particular human life memories and identity to the Spiritual Plane, a realm the soul has never really left, for the human personality, mind and memories, as well as the physical world itself, is only a dream within the soul's awareness.

We can get a glimpse of this by shutting one's physical eyes and clearing the mind, making it possible to be quietly aware of the true formlessness of the human mind's dark interior. It is in reality, a window to the void of eternity. The darkness within is not in the shape of the inside of a human skull at all, rather, it is a vast, dimensionless, fathomless void.

The soul does not occupy a specific position in this void; the soul *is* the infinite inner mind itself. It is The Dreamer, dreaming of a human life experience within its own awareness. The human personality, whose awareness, is a mixture of soul awareness plus the habitual mind's (ego) recorded past, is not real. When the human body deceases and is no more, the soul is compelled to take this record of human life with it as the soul is in reality the human awareness itself, freed from the constraints of the ego.

Whilst on the Physical Plane simulating a human life, the soul's self awareness is what is referred to on the Spiritual Plane as 'Unknowing'. When on the Spiritual Plane, the soul's self awareness is referred to as 'Knowing'. A soul does not and cannot move from where its awareness eternally is, for all that it consists of is awareness and no-thing else.

At the death of the human body, (the outer, physical shell of the soul, so to speak) a soul's self awareness remains constant and lucid as it transitions instantly from 'Unknowing' to 'Knowing'- realizing immediately that it is and always has been the One Awareness in the nothingness of eternity.

Not only does Sol have the capability to transition from 'Unknowing' to 'Knowing' at the end of each human lifetime, he can and does do so, on a regular basis during the current lifetime. When the human body is asleep, Sol's self awareness transitions from

'Unknowing' on the Physical Plane to 'Knowing' on the Spiritual Plane.

This is an important ability for all souls to have, for to spend 24/7 in a human body for a full lifetime would be quite stressful. The human body is heavy and awkward, dank, humid and unwieldy compared to the lightness of the soul, making it quite uncomfortable.

While Sol is 'Knowing' on the Spiritual Plane, he catches up with his spiritual family. They include both the ones whose life experiences have come to an end (in physical terms, their body has died) but also, the ones that are still experiencing a life simulation are there to greet him too.

There is one soul in particular that he loves to reunite with. Complementing Sol in both body and spirit is his Soul Mate. Spiritually, they have been together for eternity – In body, they sometimes share a lifetime together if their agendas coincide and if not, their lifetimes are spent separate from each other in another time and place on the Physical Plane.

In the Oneness of the Spiritual Plane though, they can never be apart for they are really one and the same soul. When simulating a human life in the 'Unknowingness' of the Physical Plane, there is the illusion that they are separate, making it a joy to meet each time they are 'Knowing' on the Spiritual Plane.

Sol's Soul Mate is not separate from Sol but rather a complementary opposite, where one expression of Sol remains unseen, or hidden, which is known on the Physical Plane as feminine and the other expression of Sol remains visible, or manifest, which is known on the Physical Plane as masculine.

On the Physical Plane these two expressions of the one soul is known as Yin-Yang, a primitive truth that was purposely leaked across the imaginary divide from the Spiritual Plane to the Physical Plane as a hint of the true Oneness of reality.

Sexuality is nonexistent in the Oneness of the Spiritual Plane; it only exists in the dualistic dream of physical life, where the two expressions of a soul - the hidden (female) and the manifest (male) - are used as an attraction between the different species for the purpose of reproduction; ensuring the survival of all creatures, not just the human being.

Sol had a preference for experiencing only male simulations, while his Soul Mate preferred the female simulations. Neither of them had experienced a lifetime of a sexual orientation other than what they preferred, but many other souls sometimes swapped their sexual preferences.

If a soul was to decide to experience a life with opposite sexual genders – so as to learn specific lessons for evolutionary advancement, in both a spiritual and physical sense, or for the learning experience itself, then usually both expressions of that one soul would swap, each then living out a human life of an opposite sex to what was their norm.

This is manifested on the Physical Plane as homosexuality, where the leanings of both expressions of the soul/soul mate (Yin-Yang) are reversed so as to live out a life with opposing sexual genders.

Sometimes the simulated lifetimes openly expressed these sexual tendencies and sometimes they were repressed, but always the human self felt very uncomfortable with the sex of their body, unconsciously wishing to return to the sexual genders their soul/soul mate was used to.

Mostly though, souls simulated lifetimes of the sexual nature they preferred. It was only on these special learning curves that some chose to live out such one off lifetimes. On the Spiritual Plane it made no difference to the soul, for all souls are 'sexless' so to speak.

While Sol was 'Knowing' on the Spiritual Plane, he eagerly looked forward to spending time with his Soul Mate, continuing to play out the roles of male and female as was their preference and as they had done in many prior human life simulations.

For although the Physical Plane was set up by Yahweh to experience Himself in form using the dualistic contrasts of opposites, there were also facilities on the Spiritual Plane itself where this delightful pastime could continue.

Experiencing physical life was stressful for the souls. Even after countless simulations, it never seemed to get any easier. The heaviness and humidity of the body itself, the ego's constant chattering and negative thoughts was all a strain. That was the main reason souls transitioned to the 'Knowing' of the Spiritual Plane when the human was sleeping.

It was a much needed break from the pain and drama of physical life. While the human was asleep and the soul was 'Knowing', the simulator would switch to automatic and the sensory receptors that were normally attached to the soul would be desensitized.

During sleep, the ego would often randomly search through recent past data and sometimes review possible scenarios. On the Physical Plane, this was known as dreaming - In reality it was a dream within The Dream - These human dreams were usually quite pleasant and occasionally even erotic, causing the human to sometimes try and recreate the dream - an attempt that was usually unsuccessful.

Every now and then when Sol was absent, the temptation became too strong for Egor to resist and he would try and take over the simulation. His vain attempts at connecting to the sensory receptors caused havoc within the simulator and the human's habitual mind would become uncontrollable.

On the Physical Plane, this was known as a nightmare, where the human self became very much agitated and scared. This sent a signal to Sol on the Spiritual

Plane, who then had to hurry back to the simulator and take back control from Egor, who sometimes remained reluctant to let go and return to his proper station. Once Sol was reconnected he immediately became 'Unknowing' and thus woke up startled and full of fear until the human self finally realized it was only a dream - albeit a bad one.

Although the human sleep time was of a fairly short duration, time did not exist on the Spiritual Plane, therefore there was no limits placed on Sol's stay there. If no alarm bells rang signifying Egor's meddling, he would not return until well refreshed. This was where Sol could spend quality Rest and Recreation with his Soul Mate.

Although there was only the One Dream there were three levels to that One Dream. First of all there was the lower level, the Physical Plane. This was the most important level really as it was created to allow the souls the ability to experience the contrasts between positive and negative forces, good and evil etc.

The Spiritual Plane was the middle level. It acted as a meeting point for all souls, where they met to discuss their different agendas and to assemble souls together in groups, selected for their appropriateness to assist with the learning experiences of each other's agendas on any upcoming physical life simulation.

They could also advise and assist in the progress of a physical life that was still active. The Spiritual Plane was also there to allow souls to reunite with loved ones that had transitioned to 'Knowing' at the end of their human life simulation.

There was also a third level where souls could rest and relax in perfect love, joy and peace. It was known as the 'Heavenly Plane'. On this level, unlike on the Physical Plane, nothing was dying, there was no such thing as death, everything was fresh and healthy, colourful and vibrantly alive. There was no disease, no pain and no negative emotions.

A soul had the ability to create whatever environment they liked on the Heavenly Plane, including an Earthly one. Whatever they could possibly imagine, they were free to create for their total enjoyment. There were no restrictions, only the freedom to be and do whatever they wished, and being timeless, for as long as they wished.

Sol though, had a soft spot for Earth, for even with all the brutality and conflict, death and destruction that overwhelmed the planet, he understood there was a purpose to it all – and underneath the pall of violence and negativity, it was still a beautiful world – after all, it was created by The Creator.

Sol and Mae (who was his Soul Mate) enthusiastically created this perfect Earth in its pristine glory on the Heavenly Plane to enjoy between human simulations and during human sleep time. They both eagerly looked forward to those very special, heavenly occasions.

Heaven was greatly misconstrued on the Physical Plane, mainly caused by the brainwashing of religious dogma. This was understandable, for the ego happened to be in control of the minds who devised and perpetuated this dogma - so mistakenly it was thought that if a heaven existed at all, it was only accessible to the chosen few who were so called 'pious, good and deserving' - but that was not so.

All souls, no matter what their human persona was or had been, basked in the joyfulness of the Heavenly Plane more often than they suffered the rigors of the

Physical Plane. As the Heavenly Plane was free of time, or any other physical constraint, they could be who or whatever they wished.

Sol and Mae chose ethereal human bodies as the vehicle of choice for their stays in heaven. They were content for its weightlessness in spirit was like wearing a suit of fine gossamer compared to the leaden dankness of the physical body that felt to them like they were having a lukewarm bath while wearing a heavy trench coat.

This spiritual human body was never hungry or thirsty and yet nourishment of any sort could be freely and eagerly savoured without risk of obesity or disease – or hangovers. Chocolate, ice cream, sweets, alcohol, all that wonderfully naughty stuff could be enjoyed guiltlessly and endlessly, without the harmful side effects which resulted from over indulgence on the Physical Plane.

This was paradise; this was what it was all about. After a soul experienced a human lifetime of negativities and hardships on the Physical Plane, contrasting them with the positives and ease of the Heavenly

Plane, eternal spiritual existence could be properly and fully appreciated.

That was why the Physical Plane was there - and needed to remain there - as an important level of The Dream. That was where the hard work was done. That's where souls needed to revisit often, to regularly experience the negative contrasts of a human lifetime.

But now Sol and Mae were in Heaven for a well earned rest, and thoughts of human life on the Physical Plane were far from their mind. Moonlight seamlessly superseded the light of the setting sun, casting a subdued luminescence over the duskiness of twilight. Glisten tipped wavelets raced each other towards the shore of Paradise Island, eager to show Sol and Mae the way as they strolled arm in arm along its idyllic foreshore.

They left no footprints in the sand as their ethereal human bodies were light as a feather. They had no need for speech, for words were only constructs used on the Physical Plane, although Sol and Mae did choose to talk some times, for they liked to say how much they loved each other as they did while on Earth.

They had made love earlier, for even though propagation of the species did not apply on the Heavenly Plane, the act of love making was the greatest gift that soul mates could give each other. The intense feelings of sexual climax in heaven made its Physical Plane counterpart seem mediocre at the least.

They found a grassy knoll amongst the swaying palms and happily settled down as they quietly drank in the pristine beauty of this heavenly island. Sol began to think about the simulated human life he was presently experiencing and how different it was to what he was feeling at the moment.

When Sol was Unknowing he firmly believed he was the Egor of the human personality he was simulating, yet when he was 'Knowing' like now on the Heavenly Plane, sitting blissfully with his eternal love, he clearly saw the mindlessness of his pseudo identity.

Because of this intermittent identity crisis, he knew this was where Egor would love to be, but to him it was all conjecture, he had never seen it and never would, for Egor was of the physical world - a part of the Physical Plane dream.

He was sentenced to one single lifetime on the Physical Plane. There he would remain until death and then he would be no more, for that was where he was meant to be and what he was meant to do. Egor provided the contrasts that the Physical Plane was created for - and whilst ever Sol believed he was Egor - Sol got to experience these negativities first hand.

Sol and Mae were there at the beginning when Yahweh (God) first desired to create a physical universe with Earth as its centrepiece and both had played a significant role in early experiments, simulating many different types of primitive creatures, culminating with what was called, the Great Ape.

Yahweh decided that a refined version of the ape might be a suitable vehicle for the souls to get around in on the Physical Plane, so they began piloting different prototypes, ending up with the final design of what was to be called Man.

They felt privileged for Yahweh had given them the opportunity to play a vital role in the opening sequence of mankind's drama of life on Earth. Sol was to play a human called Adam and Mae was to play his companion, Eve.

They were to be the first of the simulated humans in their final form - it also happened to be one of the rare occasions Sol and Mae had the chance to share a lifetime together in the same human life drama. All was new to them as they hesitantly experienced their first simulation in the new improved PSPR.

The Garden of Eden had always existed on the Heavenly Plane and was simply copied and pasted to the Physical Plane as a basis for starting off the drama of human life. It was not intended to be the idyllic paradise that Sol and Mae were used to in heaven.

Yahweh's re-creation of the Garden on Earth came as a shock to Sol and Mae and to make it worse, Yahweh had introduced an updated, more advanced Egor as part of the simulation, to provide the human persona needed for the soul's experience. They had known of and interacted with the primitive Egor before, but this one was a real *Doozy!*

On Paradise Island, Sol and Mae were reminiscing about their early simulations when Sol received an alarm from his PSPR informing him that the simulation was waking. Mae would wait for him there as she was between lives, for her last simulation had died in a car crash some four years before. Sol kissed her gently and headed back to the Unknowing of the Physical Plane.

* * *

SULLY lay spreadeagled on the hard stony ridge overlooking a desolate valley in Afghanistan. His platoon was stretched out either side of him. They could not see the Taliban, but they could hear them as their rifle fire came in irregular staccato bursts aimed in the general direction of Sully and his men. The heat was oppressive, the humidity stifling and the hordes of blood sucking flies unbearable.

Twenty seven year old platoon sergeant Ben Sullivan, better known to all as Sully, was leading his men on a sortie into No Man's Land, hopefully to wipe out the Taliban contingent firmly ensconced amongst the sand dunes and sparse vegetation on the far side of the ridge. At the moment, the Dune Coons were winning.

Sully believed in what he was doing. He had volunteered after the love of his life, Mia, had been killed in a car accident some four years earlier. He had lost both her and the will to live, but rather than drown his sorrows in alcohol or worse, he decided to head for the war torn areas of the world and see if he could make a difference.

His Dad had died when he was nineteen, which came as a devastating blow for Sully, but eventually he got over it only to lose his Mum later on. At least with his Mum, they knew it was coming. She was diagnosed with terminal breast cancer some six months before, whereas his father had died suddenly from a heart attack.

"Bloody stinking, camel rooting Arabs" he muttered to himself, "they're all alike, you can't trust any of the bastards." Based at Tarinkot, he was eating breakfast just before going on patrol when Sully heard the news from headquarters that some arsehole suicide bomber had blown himself up in Kabul, taking a pile of civilians and a couple of Sully's army mates with him.

There was another suicide bombing in Baghdad the day before that took out eight Iraqi policemen and two Yank engineers. Sully had been stationed in Iraq before being posted here and it was a tossup which hellhole was worse. Sully heard the 'Towel Heads' jabbering in the distance, they were preparing for another onslaught.

Reluctantly, Sully admitted to himself that he had maybe met a few decent Towel Heads during his time here, but they were few and far between. Most of them were dick heads brainwashed by those bloody, shit lickin' Pakis over the border. They were the ones that harboured and protected those mongrel, Islamic fundamentalist pricks. "The Pakis should be exterminated too," he mused.

'Zing'- a bullet screamed across the gap between Sully and Bazza, the soldier to his left. Sully looked across in trepidation, Bazza wasn't moving. "Christ, he's been shot!" Bazza, better known to his parents as Barry, had become one of Sully's best mates after they were stationed together at Camp Victory in Baghdad.

Suddenly Bazza lifted a weary hand to brush away a swarm of those god forsaken flies and Sully heaved a sigh of relief. Most of the rifle fire from the Dune Coons pinged off into the wild blue yonder as their weapons were mostly antiquated and they were usually poor shots, this time they had missed again thank Christ, luck was on their side.

Sully never heard the shot that killed him. Out of the blue, seemingly in slow motion, his chest exploded in a bright crimson spray. "What the hell? Who's blood's that all over me?... Christ! Is it mine... have I been friggin' shot?... I'm dying... Christ Almighty!"

Suddenly a spasm of terror spread through Sully's body like an icy tornado as he realized that this was the day he thought would never come - not here, not in this god forsaken arsehole of a country. But it looked as though his number had come up; he had a sudden sense of dread that he was well and truly stuffed!

Then he stood up, feeling slightly light headed, "well, maybe I'm not dead after all" he murmured still in shock. Sully looked down at the crumpled, bloodied body that lay motionless on the ground in front of him. "Poor bastard" he thought out aloud, "looks as though he's well and truly buggered... Wait a minute... isn't that's me?"

Sully/Sol took one last look at the dusty, barren battleground where Sully's Unknowing was ending and quietly and smoothly transitioned to the Knowing of the Spiritual Plane.

Mission successful squawked the intercom, simulation complete, preparing for computer shutdown, standing by for Egor decommissioning. Sol's PSPR was now in automatic mode. It would be reformatted and then reprogrammed for the next human life simulation. Sol/ Sully had transitioned to the Spiritual Plane

It was this PSPR that Sol had been piloting when spending time with Mae on Paradise Island while the simulation was asleep in his barracks at TaranKot, Afghanistan on the last night before Sully's final day of Unknowing on Earth. When Sully stirred, Sol returned to the Physical Plane to complete his mission.

Everyone was there to greet Sully. He was still bewildered as he fumbled with the reality of it all. He was supposed to be dead and yet, here he was alive and kicking. "Who's that over there in the crowd?" A familiar face thought Sully... "Well I'll be buggered, it's Dad, I don't believe it... it's been such a long time since I've seen him... and there's Mum standing by his side with a big grin on her face. Shit! It's just not possible."... But it was.

Sully hurried across to his parents and tenderly but hesitantly embraced them both, something he thought he would never do again. "It's all over Ben" his father said softly, "your mission is complete, you don't have to suffer the pain anymore - you're home at last."

All the people that were ever important to him were there to greet Sully. The ones like his Mum and Dad that had died before him, plus all his other loving friends that had also previously passed on. Plus many others that were still alive on Earth, all his army mates, including Bazza. They were all there - everyone.

Sully was surprised to see that even some enemy Towel Heads were there. Then he remembered they were souls too, helping him to complete his mission, in fact, he recalled that he had arranged for them to play a part in his life drama before he began the Sully lifetime simulation. Not only were some of the Towel Heads decent blokes he realized - they all were.

He was also a little surprised that his identity remained intact. His awareness of himself as Ben Sullivan and his past never dissolved into Sol. He realized then he had always been Sol - the Unknowing Sol. - Plus all his negativities, including his anger and hatred for his fellow man had dissipated, they had been left behind on the battlefield with the now redundant Egor.

Sully's attention was caught by the most beautiful, yet familiar face in the crowd. He could not believe his eyes, it was his long lost love Mia, waiting in the background for Sully to come to terms with what was happening to him. He raced over to her and although his body was now light as a feather, his steps were heavy with emotion.

To Sully, all his Christmases had come at once. Sully/Sol took Mia/Mae into his aching, loving arms and tenderly kissed her on her soft sweet lips. It really did feel like heaven to Sully as they tenderly touched and caressed each other.

This was Sully's time. This was a souls whole purpose for living a human lifetime on the Physical Plane. The rewards were being handed out and Sully was the eager and deserving recipient. This was also Sol's time. He had transitioned to the Knowing every time Sully's simulator was sleeping, but he always left his Unknowing behind with Sully on the Physical Plane.

Now that Sully's simulation was in progress, Sol was both Knowing and Unknowing, but this final time, his Unknowing had followed him to the Spiritual Plane. Sol's Knowing had dissolved Sully's Unknowing and Sully's Heavenly journey could now begin.

Even when physical evolution reaches a stage where mankind is mature enough to handle 'Knowing' (God's ultimate plan for The Dream) the Physical Plane will still be needed. When man fully realizes there is no separation, only Oneness, man's violence and cruelty against man and other living creatures will end, but there will still be a need for contrasts to be made.

Sol and Mae understood that life on Earth was not meant to be perfect or easy. It became evident that every human body on Earth was meant to sicken and die. Human relationships, governments, religious institutions, machines and even Earth's weather patterns are all meant to fail.

Death, disease and natural disasters are all essential elements of Earth's makeup. While 'Unknowing', they have continually tried to make the imperfect perfect, the horrible beautiful and the limited limitless and each time they have failed miserably. Earth is in the same negative shape today as it was when they first began human simulations.

Whilst 'Unknowing' that is a very difficult truth to come to terms with, but so simple to understand when 'Knowing'. Every transition they make to the Spiritual Plane brings a sudden, startling awareness of the commonsense and purpose of it all, it is all wonderfully meant to be.

After Sully's Physical Plane simulation ended, he came to understand that he was now experiencing the Heavenly Plane Dream, not the Physical Plane Dream – although in truth, both dreams are part of The One Dream.

The difference is that on the Heavenly Plane, the Physical Plane environment is reproduced in all its perfection - without such thing as death, or pain, disease or natural disasters - no negativities at all. This was a soul's eternal reward for a life on Earth. Sully realized he was not in a Heaven on Earth so to speak, but rather an 'Earth in Heaven' - and it was beautiful – and absolutely wonderful.

Sully would continue to experience his own identity eternally. The dualistic framework of form on the Physical Plane is an illusion that causes mankind to appear to be separate from each other, enabling the diversity of life experiences that are needed for our soul's progress. Thus while Sully was enjoying his heavenly journey with Mia, Sol began making arrangements to move on.

That would seem impossible as Sol is Sully, so he would have to be where Sully was, but on the Spiritual Plane, that is not the case. Sully's separate identity may have begun by being forged in finite flesh on the Physical Plane, but at the same time, his identity was delivered and consecrated in the Oneness of Yahweh (God) on the Spiritual Plane.

Sol began to arrange for his next trip in a new PSPR. A soul often referred to this as preparing to go *'down'* to Hell, for Earth is better known on the Spiritual Plane as Hell. The same when they transitioned to the Spiritual Plane, souls sometimes referred to it as going *'up'* to Heaven (from a hell on Earth).

This reference was misinterpreted on the Physical Plane, becoming a myth to mean that hell was somewhere *'down'* there, which became even more exaggerated over time (because of the oppressiveness of the human body and earthly environment) as a hot world full of fire and brimstone, with a nasty devil waiting to stick a pitchfork into the bum of any soul that had the misfortune to be bad whilst alive.

Conversely, if they were good, they would go *'up'* to heaven, somewhere above. This myth was spread mainly by religious doctrine to allay the fears of the believers of their own particular faiths, each faith having a different interpretation, but it was complete and utter baloney.

In reality, there is nowhere one can go. What the souls were referring to when they said go *'up'* to heaven meant to go up in awareness, to go up in consciousness, to become enlightened - to 'Know'. The same applies in the reverse. To go *'down'* to hell meant to go down in awareness, to go down from consciousness to unconsciousness, to regress to un-enlightenment – to 'Unknowingness'.

Sol's next human life plan was quite involved, as it was with the Sully simulation. It must have a clearly defined objective, yet allow Sol total free will.

The simulation would include a complete human personality based on the lessons Sol had already learned, plus the ones he had yet to learn. There needed to be a set of goals to be accomplished, challenges to be overcome, fears to be faced, and experiences to be gained.

Firstly, Sol needed to review what he had yet to learn and experience, then gather the souls around him who could supply the necessary skills and attributes to simulate the people that would closely interact with him during his human lifetime, plus those who would play the part of his foes, antagonists and maybe even his killer, for although Sol had experienced violence in his lifetimes, there was still much to learn.

Sol's main regret was that he would once again have to contend with Egor. Although Sol hated to admit it, Egor was a necessary evil for a human life simulation - but still, Sol didn't have to like it – or him.

Earth is a classroom and its students are souls. It really isn't much different to a human classroom, in that it consists of an average mix of souls from differing levels of learning. This is the same degree of intelligence spread amongst the human population on Earth.

All souls were pure and positive when 'Knowing' but whilst they were 'Unknowing' a soul was at risk of being completely overwhelmed by Egor (their ego), causing them to become distracted. This could cause them to fail a life test, thus requiring them to repeat further lifetimes at the same level until they passed.

It was the souls that failed their missions on Earth themselves who decided to repeat class, not Yahweh, as he was a compassionate and understanding teacher. Most times, those souls who had failed a life lesson would forgo time on the Heavenly Plane, opting instead to go back to Earth immediately, to endeavour to learn the lessons assigned to them. The reason they were so keen to learn was that the ultimate aim of all souls was to advance to the level of Yahweh.

Every single human being on earth, whether they are so called good or bad, transitions to the Spiritual Plane when they die, every one of them, for in reality there are no bad people. All so called badness is only the negativity that is used as a learning tool to contrast against the positives that all souls enjoy in their true home in Heaven.

Yahweh's ultimate purpose for Creation and the end rewards that souls aspired to when they learned to overcome all negativities, filtered through to the mind of man as a religious objective, *'To be as Christ and sit on the right hand side of God.'* To reach that pinnacle though, souls had to experience every facet of human life, especially the negativities, which could be separated into two main categories.

Firstly 'Physical Violence'- which includes experiencing anything from extreme hardship, physical pain, accidents, disabilities, disease, natural disasters, crime of all types, cruelty, murder, rape, torture, paedophilia, war etc. All physical violence must be experienced both as the victim and as the perpetrator.

Secondly, 'Mental Violence' - this includes greed, envy, lust, pride, vanity, spite, arrogance, selfishness, rage and much, much more. Again mental violence must be experienced both as possessing those negative traits and also while being on the receiving end. Souls must learn from the experience of all negativities before they can advance along the pathway to enlightenment - and to Yahweh.

If a lesson is not learned, that lesson will be repeated again and again in further lives until it is. Until then the soul will be 'stuck' on the same level of 'Unknowing'. Some souls needed only one lifetime to learn the lessons assigned for that life, so were more advanced in the learning experience than other souls.

There was no hurry for slow learners to catch up, as the Spiritual Plane was timeless and in reality, all souls were equal - except when 'Unknowing' while learning the lessons assigned to them during a human lifetime on the Physical Plane - plus there was another incentive.

Yahweh often needed souls from both ends of the learning spectrum to perform special lifetime missions on the Physical Plane and all souls aspired to be chosen for such missions.

Apart from souls needing to undergo negative life experiences, both physical and mental, in their journey towards enlightenment, they also need to experience human body dysfunctions of all kinds, including eating disorders such as obesity and anorexia, plus all the other illnesses, dis-eases, (which means 'the body is not at ease') maladies and deformities that affect the physical human body.

In truth they are all lessons of life, so are really blessings in disguise, a truth not understood by the 'Unknowing' human mind. The average soul can work through these sufferings fairly quickly, maybe a lifetime for each disorder, but if there are specific lessons to be learned, perhaps carried over from lessons not learned in past lives, a soul may need more than one lifetime to work through and overcome them.

Once each disorder is experienced and conquered however, a soul never needs to suffer that disability again. There is nothing faulty with the inhabiting soul or the human being who is experiencing these disabilities. Only the physical body suffers - and the body is an illusion - a part of The Dream.

The soul that inhabits the physical body has always been and always will be perfect. It is this soul awareness within the human body that transitions to the 'Knowing' of the Spiritual Plane, not the physical body itself. All 'Unknowing' human beings are in reality, whole and perfect in every way, their sick and failing physical bodies or minds are simply the vehicle through which lessons are to be learned.

Whenever Yahweh decided a special mission was warranted to assist man in some way, or to provide lessons that needed to be experienced and learned, a special classroom was allocated in which Yahweh gathered a collective of souls that all needed to learn that same particular lesson or lessons.

Sometimes these missions were to provide benevolent pointers that would assist mankind in his evolution on the road to enlightenment and sometimes they were to provide lessons that would expose certain groups of souls to sometimes horrific, negative experiences.

Benevolent simulations have occurred many times since Creation, most notably with the simulation of a human being named Jesus. Not the Jesus of religious doctrine, where he has been misrepresented to the extreme, but the real Jesus. The human Jesus was as 'Unknowing' as any other human being, but Yahweh had certain doorways in his mind purposely left slightly ajar.

When the time was right, this allowed an advanced soul named Christ, the pilot of the Jesus simulation, to experience the physical drama on Earth whilst 'Knowing' rather than 'Unknowing' and as there is really only 'Oneness' it was in fact Yahweh who directly shared the awareness of the human Jesus. Jesus then had knowledge of what the average human could never understand and during his time on Earth, he imparted Yahweh's insightful teachings to all who would listen.

His teachings have also filtered through the ages as continual signposts pointing towards what mankind needs to do - and yet few heed that advice. When Jesus' physical body died, it decomposed back into the earth as all other finite bodies do; it was his spiritual body (his Christ soul) that transitioned to the Spiritual Plane.

Jesus was a simulated human like any other, who apart from his mission to deliver Yahweh's timely messages to mankind also had an agenda to fulfil. He needed to experience the negativities of the Physical Plane that he had not yet experienced, hence his abuse at the hands of the Romans, and his subsequent torture, culminating in his extreme experience of physical negativity when he was nailed to a cross.

As it was with all souls who experience physical life and death, Jesus' separate identity began by being forged in finite flesh on the Physical Plane, but at the same time his identity, cloaked in his spiritual body was delivered to the Oneness of Yahweh and eternity on the Spiritual Plane.

Jesus' separate, self awareness continues eternally and because he is one of the more advanced souls, who have learned to conquer all physical negativities, he does in fact sit on the right hand side of Yahweh. He is also known on Earth as Christ, but in reality He is the 'Knowing' soul within all mankind.

Occasionally, certain groups of souls needed to experience and conquer an extremely negative human life drama. In these instances, Yahweh would gather a collective together that had not been exposed to this type of experience before or had failed the lesson previously, then choose a teacher, the same way as he had chosen a soul to simulate the human Jesus.

All souls that had not experienced this particular human life drama before are invited to participate. It is completely voluntary of course but every soul must eventually experience and conquer all Physical Plane negativities extreme or not, if they want to advance along the pathway to enlightenment and to Yahweh.

There is much extreme negativity, but one that stands out in mankind's modern history is the crime of racial persecution. There is no such classification as racial ethnicity on the Spiritual Plane. All souls are equally the same, so the learning group only becomes classified by race or creed for the sake of the earthly lessons that these souls need to learn.

To fully experience persecution, Yahweh chose souls to portray a group that was known as the 'Jewish people' as the core nucleus, whose Physical Plane ancestry can be traced back to earlier human simulations of the patriarchs Abraham, Isaac and Jacob in the second millennium of the drama of mankind's journey towards enlightenment.

For the teacher, Yahweh needed to elect a soul that had failed to conquer this type of negativity on many previous life occasions, making him eligible to portray the malevolent human figure that was needed. Unlike Jesus though, this time the doors of the human mind would be kept tightly shut, giving Egor almost complete control of the simulation.

To add to the drama, the chosen soul was instructed to urge Egor into even more tyrannical behaviour than normal, by infusing sadistic malice into the nature of Egor's habitual stupidity. Although the soul was chosen by Yahweh to act as the perpetrator in the negative life drama, the soul always had the free will to learn compassion for his fellow man instead of brutality, which would have changed the course of human history.

The simulation used to demonstrate the negativity of racial persecution in this particular drama was a human named Adolf Hitler. Mankind may be abhorred by the cruelty and violence perpetrated by such a heinous villain, but on the Spiritual Plane, there is no blame, this soul was only playing a role for the purpose of learning as well as teaching.

This is incomprehensible to the habitual human mind – even though it is that very same mind that is the cause of crimes such as persecution. Other souls were also chosen to play the villain. In previous lives they had all been easily overcome and hoodwinked by Egor's wily ways, thus failing to conquer such negativities.

Human simulations such as Göring, Goebbles, Himmler and Hess, would, like Hitler after physical death, all return to Hell (Earth) for quite a few more lifetimes until they learned what they must learn, for even while acting the part of villain, they always had the free will to change for the better, learning compassion for their fellow man instead of inhumanity.

This was part of Yahweh's test for them – and as history shows – they all failed miserably. The future human life simulations that these souls would be involved in (of their own free will) would be to experience persecution as the victim instead of perpetrator, so as to experience 'the other side of the coin' so to speak.

These repeat lives would continue for them until they learned to conquer their sadistic affinity for inhumanity and brutality, replacing those negative influences with natural acts of kindness and compassion. Once learnt, these souls would never have to experience such negativity again.

As for the victims of persecution, although it is impossible for the human mind to understand, valuable lessons were presented to them during their life of trial and tribulation. It was up to each soul whether they learnt what was needed or not – if not, they, of their own free will, would elect to be subjected to similar negative experiences in future lifetimes.

> "Our aim is not for a peaceful state of mind but for a peaceful state of intelligence that questions life and its meaning."

THE AMIABLE REAPER

THE subject that most consistently crops up in life is its opposite, death. We are constantly bombarded by news about death, due to war, violence, murder, accidents, disease, sickness, old age etc. And the more gruesome or unusual it is, the more it attracts publicity. There is no greater topic to grab our undivided attention and fuel gossip mongers tongues than the news of a human death.

The media, our friends, family, people in the street, ourselves included, can't wait to discuss death. Statements such as, "Did you hear that so and so died last night?" or the even more dramatic, "Ooh! Did you hear about that terrible disaster that killed so many people?" We all like to be the first to spread such *juicy* tit-bits of information such as the death of someone.

The thought of death is always lurking somewhere in our subconscious - the impending death of ourselves especially - but also of others dear to us. For most of us it's cause for fear - fear of the unknown. A fear we can manage as long as it is someone else who is doing the dying.

But what exactly is death? What happens to us when we die? Where do we go? Most importantly, do we remain conscious of the 'self' we are accustomed to after our earthly demise? Those questions cannot be answered with any surety by anyone alive and no one has ever come back to tell us what happens.

This *unknown* is what causes the fear we experience when thinking about our own death, the fear of hell with its fire and brimstone and Satan with his pitchfork, worse still, the terrifying thought of not existing at all, of oblivion, a fear that originally conjured up the myth that there was a Grim Reaper waiting somewhere in the darkness to grab us when we die.

Death is inevitable for us all of course, but is it really to be feared or is it the stuff of legend. Could it be that death is in reality, a release, a freedom of self, loosened from the mortal cocoon we call our body and the associated constraints of physical life? Could it be that only our ego dies - that personal identity within that we only *think* we are? Is it our ego that is doing all the fearing?

Death doesn't appear to be the 'Grim Reaper' that we have been indoctrinated to believe, but rather an 'Amiable Reaper'. A synopsis of authors on the subject of death seem to point to the premise that when we die, if we are greeted by anyone at all, it will be by a loving and affectionate spirit more akin to a guardian angel than some malevolent, nasty old entity.

It is possible that it could be one of our loved ones who have previously passed or even our true spiritual self that is waiting there to guide us, but we can be reassured that a skeletal figure carrying a large scythe and clothed in a raggedy black cloak with a hood is waiting to escort us to some spiritual halfway house to await judgment is nothing but the work of folklore.

When the myth of the Grim Reaper first appeared, mankind was still lost in the dark ages. We have come a long way since then and yet we continue to hang on to this ancient notion. This belief is perpetuated mainly by religious institutions as a scaremongering tool. "Be good and follow our particular creed or the Grim Reaper will come and damn you to a life in hell" is a mantra sure to 'keep the flocks in order' so to speak.

It seems to be only our physical self, not our awareness of self that ceases to exist. When death occurs our spiritual or true self awakens from the dream of the physical world to the reality of an eternal spiritual existence. Believing we are our ego is the cause of our fear of death, for our ego does indeed cease to exist at the end of physical life, but that isn't who we really are.

All research on near death experiences seem to point towards an amiable feeling of love, joy and peace, a state of oneness that can only be described as heavenly. The term 'near-death' is a misnomer because the evidence suggests that people actually journey beyond death during near-death experiences. Philosophically, to say that such experiences are 'near-death' is like saying a woman is 'near-pregnant'.

Either a woman is pregnant or she is not. In the same way, it would seem that a person is either dead or they aren't. Near Death Experiences seem to suggest that death is not such a grim experience after all, but rather an amiable return to our true abode, a spiritual home of unconditional Love, Joy and Peace from which we have never truly left, only in a dream.

Why does death frighten us, and even though it scares us, why are we so curious about it? What is the attraction that death holds over us? Our fascination and fear of death has its roots in the fear of the unknown, or more specifically, fear of the unremembered. Even if life is full of awful experiences, trials and tribulations, we are accustomed to it. Life is familiar, mundane, known, so it isn't frightening.

We attempt to control life but our efforts are in vain, it only gives the illusion that life is tameable, while death, it's seemingly opposite, it's wild and untameable. We are so busy trying to control life, to steer along life's pathway, the way we think it should go, that we remain unconscious of the fact that life is not more manageable than death at all. It is even less ordered than death really.

Life surprises us every moment, the boundaries of our everyday existence are always shifting, and yet we are not as frightened of life as we are of death. We feel safe because we think we know life and have collectively agreed to ignore the fact that nothing stays the same. Each of us changes every moment of every day and every night. We never meet the world with the same self.

Life is just as untamed as death. But because we always look for the known and the familiar in our life, we do not consciously experience the newness of every moment. We miss the opportunity for new life as it arises, unless of course, we can face death without fear.

Death is not the grim reaper at all; its life that is grim. Death is a release from the pain and stress of life; at the end of which our soul 'chills out' in the realm we call death - until the next lifetime. Life and death are not separate, but continuations of the same spectrum of ideas. Alternating from one to the other, they form the totality of our dreams.

By breaking free of our ignorance of both life and death, and remembering the truth, we can live the lives we desire. By embracing death right now, we can actually change our lives – and the world. It is your world, your dream. Both your life and death are ever continuing, ever ongoing, complimentary parts of that dream world.

The personality that thinks it knows itself is the 'you' that lives constantly in the shadow of death. That 'You' is your ego, which is only the accumulated residue of your past memories. Your ego does in fact end and so does your body, for they are part and parcel of this finite physical world.

The attempted delaying of death, or the futile wish for immortality, comes from the mistaken belief that you are your ego, therefore you fear the end of this personality you think you are, with all its accumulated memories." But that is not the way it is at all. Death should be welcomed when it arrives. It is the release from the confines of physical life to the remembrance of who you really are, a free spirit playing at being a human being for awhile.

It is not so much that something (Grim or Amiable) is waiting for us when we die, but that death itself is kindly, a welcome and joyful event when our time comes. A time when we will remember who we really are and why we decided to spend a short lifetime in the physical world. Death really is a life changing experience and if we can remember what death truly is before we die, then we will face it without fear.

Ever since human beings were introduced into the 'The Story of the Universe', we have remained relatively ignorant of why we and everything else in the universe exists. Who are we? What are we supposed to be doing? What is the purpose of it all? Why should the universe and all that's in it bother to play out this drama of physical life if it's a onetime event for each and every one of us?

If we all have only one go at it, to live one lifetime here, one of mainly pain and suffering sprinkled with a few drops of happiness, what's our reward? We are told that we should be good, to learn to overcome evil, to aspire to greatness, but why, what incentive do we have? What reason do we have if at the end of our short stay here, its curtains - forever?

We may as well be bastards like Hitler or Osama Bin Laden or any other despot. We might as well be consumed by greed as most of our bankers, politicians and big business' are. Why try to be a better person? Does it matter one iota whether we are good or bad, compassionate or cold hearted, a Good Samaritan or a callous murderer? Maybe not, if it's oblivion waiting for us all at the end of our short stay here.

If the objective is for the survival of the species as a whole, as suggested by some experts, then, when we've done our bit, it's goodbye world, permanently, we can't ever know or be privy to the results of all our hard work and striving to be a good (or even bad) human being, which seems nonsensical and unfair, so it's bewildering why we bother to live our one life in the first place?

Unless of course, we are lucky enough to have had a glimpse of something special and realize that all is not as it seems. Is there a kind and compassionate Amiable Reaper waiting patiently for our time to depart our moral coil? Sounds good, but we'll have to wait and see.

> "Open your eyes to what is really happening, not what looks like is happening. Do not judge by outward appearances."

BLACK HOLES

THIS STORY has nothing to do with the physical structure of black holes; rather it's to illustrate the fact that we seldom take an unbiased look at anything in our lives that is in anyway strange or unusual. We tend to look at all new objects or enigmas through a cloud of past experiences, which means we don't see them for what they are at all, only an interpretation that conforms to what we already know and understand.

When confronted with anything new, we attempt to understand it using old thought patterns. We try to make it fit into a familiar slot so we can understand what it is, and when it doesn't fit, we are at a loss to explain it, like black holes for instance. Instead we concoct up an explanation that seems plausible and compatible with our very limited understanding of life.

We think in the past and these thoughts which are naturally old and stale and therefore of no real value if we are going to understand something that is completely new to our experience. To do that a new way of thinking is required. Until then, black holes will remain one of our universe's confusing anomalies.

The point is to look at everything new, or not so new in our world from different angles, not just the three dimensional angle that we have used in the past. If scientists could shake off the cobwebs of the past from their minds, maybe they could take a fresh and clear look at black holes - or anything else that is new to mankind.

It comes down to the fact that we will never learn about or understand new things while we are using old thinking methods. We need to realize and accept ourselves as being three dimensional inhabitants of a three dimensional universe and that there are maybe, other ways of thinking about things.

One way is to leave three dimensional thought out of it and think with an open mind when attempting to figure out what black holes might or might not be. Understanding them is also an inroad into understanding who we really are and why we are here in the first place.

Roughly, a black hole is the result of an exploding star many times more massive than our sun. Its gravity caves in on itself, compressing the remaining matter to such a degree that a teaspoon of it could weigh many billions of tonnes.

A black hole's escape velocity (the speed needed to escape the star's gravity) is more than the speed of light, which is approx. 300,000 km/s or 186,000 miles/s, so even light cannot escape, hence the name, black hole. In theory they are everywhere in the universe, but can't be seen of course. The Earths escape velocity on the other hand is a mere 11.186 km/s or around 25,000 m.p.h. This is the speed a spacecraft has to reach before it can escape earth's gravity and go into orbit.

In trying to understand the larger objects in the universe, we rely mostly on Einstein's theory of relativity, which is three dimensional science. For the smaller objects - atoms and the more miniscule particles, we rely mostly on quantum mechanics - three dimensional physics.

Scientific theory surmises that a black hole is cone shaped and as far as can be determine, has the top of the cone (called the event horizon) in our three dimensional space, then narrows down to a vortex at the bottom point something like a whirlpool.

The hypothesis is this bottom point would be infinitesimally small where gravity is absolute and space and time come to what has been termed as a singularity (time and space become the same). This is only speculation really for scientific formulas, devised in our three dimensional universe, come up short when trying to explain exactly what a black hole is.

Why? Because a black hole might not be just three dimensional, it could be multi-dimensional. If so, it cannot be explained by using the narrow, limited thinking of three dimensional science.

The universe as a whole and everything in it is most likely far, far more elaborate and much more magnificent than what we can understand with our limited knowledge. So if we try to understand black holes without using three dimensional thought, what then might they be and what good does it do us to know anyway?

Theoretically, black holes are everywhere in our universe with the more massive black holes at the centre of each galaxy, including our own Milky Way. Science hypothesizes that the black hole at the centre of our galaxy is some 4 million times more massive than our sun.

With an open mind, let's use our imagination to peer into the depths of a black hole. From the point of singularity at the bottom, we mentally look up the side of the black hole towards the surface, which in our case is our three dimensional space, where everything has a height, width and depth.

Now let's surmise that somewhere above the bottom point, (the singularity) there is a slot that contains a One Dimensional Universe where everything has only a height, or a width or a depth. Then, what if further up the vortex, we come to a slot that contains a Two Dimensional Universe, where everything has a combination of two of height, width or depth.

Each dimension is as complete and self-contained as our universe is, with its own galaxies, stars and planets populated by either one or two dimensional living creatures.

The inhabitants of a one dimensional world would believe that their universe was all there is and would be completely unaware of the two dimensionals and us three dimensionals above them. They would presume that the black hole's surface is in their universe. Any scientific theories that they used to try and understand black holes would be restricted to one dimensional thinking.

The inhabitants of a two dimensional world would believe that their universe was all there is and would be completely unaware of the one dimensionals below them and us three dimensionals above them. They would presume that the black hole's surface is in their universe. Any scientific theories that they used to try and understand black holes would be restricted to two dimensional thinking.

The inhabitants of our three dimensional world believe that our universe is all there is and are completely unaware of the one and two dimensionals below us. We presume that the black hole's surface is in our universe. All of our scientific theories that attempt to explain a black hole are restricted to three dimensional thinking. Are but! It does not end there.

Who's to say that a black hole stops at our universe? What if it continues on to a fourth dimensional universe, then a fifth, then a sixth dimensional universe ad infinitum! The inhabitants of all these other universes would be living their lives, experiencing all the dramas, hopes and fears of their particular world, as we do ours, completely oblivious as we are that other dimensional universes exist.

If this were true, would we be so unique or would we be just a part of something magnificently spectacular? Three dimensional beings sharing a multi-dimensional universe that contains many other varied dimensions inhabited by many other, very, very different and diverse living creatures, that would be beyond our ability to detect or understand.

We would never be able to meet, or share our science, or understand anything about each other, nor even know that the others exist. What we can do though is to become consciously aware of whom we are and the role we might be playing in this wonder of life, pondering for a moment that our universe may not be all there is.

Here, everything, including ourselves, needs to have three dimensions, a height, a width and a depth, which means that for us to recognize anything outside of our universe, it would have to have those same three dimensional qualities otherwise we would not recognize it for what it was nor even know it was there.

In this hypothetical multi-universe, imagine for a moment a further possibility. What if it was the case that all the other universes are not in reality below us or above us at all? What if they are right here around us in this one illusory space/time continuum?

Being of different dimensions, if they were sharing our space, they would be as invisible to us as we are to them. We could all be co-existing together right now, sharing this one space in this illusory multi-dimensional universe.

Astrophysicists are forever searching for missing matter in the universe. They question why there is a certain amount of mass missing that should be there to make the universe work the way it does. They have fancy names like dark matter or dark energy, anti matter etc, but where and what it is they don't really know.

The need for extra dark or invisible matter, is inferred from gravitational effects on visible matter and was originally hypothesized to account for discrepancies between the mass of galaxies and the universe as a whole, based on the mass of the visible luminous matter these objects contain, as we three dimensional beings *'know and understand it'*.

What if that anomaly could be accounted for by factoring in the extra mass contained in a multi dimensional universe - a mass that is invisible and as impossible for us three dimensionals to detect as the inside of a black hole, but is an essential component for the total mass of this multi dimensional universe?

Is the mass held in the other dimensions the 'missing matter' that our scientists are so eagerly looking for, a question that we can never answer when it is realized that the elusive matter is invisible to detection by three dimensional means?

There are many questions that arise when attempting to reason why things are the way they are, especially when they are not within our range of understanding. We need to be inspired, to think outside of the norm.

All mankind's major discoveries came as a result of inspiration - a new thought bubbles and bursts through the hard shell of conditioned thought - and something new is invented or understood. Could it be possible that a black hole is a tear in the fabric of space, exposing the universe's true reality?

For us to understand black holes or any of the universe's anomalies, we must get out of our habitual ways and think differently, then like opening a window to the breeze, the answer may come in - and then again it may not, but at least it has a chance if the window is open - it has no hope if it is closed.

> "There is no such thing as failure. Everything advances us on our evolutionary journey."

MULTIPLICITY

OUR SPACESHIP hovers perilously close to the black hole's event horizon, the point of no return. The gravitational pull is all powerful and if the ship slips over that critical point we are committed - there is no way back. It is prohibiting us from getting close enough to peer down into the vortex to see what's there.

Of course we still could take the plunge but it would be a one way trip - and we would have to be mighty quick to see what's inside for we would be travelling faster than the speed of light - before we were obliterated. However there is nothing stopping us from travelling safely and at a much more sedate speed, all we need do is use our imagination.

Last time we looked into a black hole, we witnessed different dimensional universes as we looked up the vortex walls, beginning with a one dimensional universe, then a two, then our own three dimensional universe; then a fourth, fifth and so on.

This time we are going to suppose something different from what we saw last time. We are going to imagine what we would see if The Creator had decided that three dimensions was the optimum number for the whole multi-universe.

These universes would still be infinite in number for although all matter in the physical universe is finite, there is no end to the universe itself. There always has to be another wall on the other side of a wall - there always has to be something more beyond the skies limit. There has to be another universe on the other side of every universe.

If these universes are all three dimensional, we can hypothesize that they would be virtually identical in content, in other words, replicas or clones of each other. The stars, the planets, the solar system, the earth, the land, the oceans, would all be the same. All living creatures would be identical copies of each other, existing separately and yet connectedly whilst unbeknownst to each other, on each and every dimensional level.

If we then factor in free will in this non ending, three dimensional multi-universe, it seems logical that there would also have to be an infinite number of possibilities spread across those universes.

Each dimension in this multi-dimensional universe was created the same, which means that every finite *'thing'* was copied exactly onto every level. Since the time of Creation this remains true, except for the effects of the infinite possibilities brought about by free will that causes the probability of a different outcome occurring over time on each and every one of these individual dimensional levels.

Thus, every *'thing'* is living and dying, being and not being, slightly differently on each level within that infinite universe. It stands to reason then, there must also be an infinite number of exact copies of you, me and everyone else, living separate/connected lifetimes, all completely unaware of our own multiplicity.

Unlike our experience of life, the multi-universe is timeless and space-less so these levels would not in reality be stacked one on top of the other or side by side, they would all exist in the same illusory time/space continuum - They would be all around us - and in us right now.

We can't detect them of course; it would be rather confusing and pointless if we could. We only experience the one tiny dimensional level that we are *aware* of inhabiting. It's similar to television and radio waves, the air is full of them but there would only be a confusing garble of sights and sounds if we tuned into all of them at once.

So we tune our television and radio sets to one particular frequency, so we can watch, listen and comprehend. It's the same with our existence. We exist concurrently on an infinite number of levels, but we are only tuned into this particular dimensional level, so we can live, experience and comprehend one aspect of our infinite number of human lifetimes. The one small part of us that is tuned into this particular level is our ego.

Considering that there are an infinite number of copies of ourselves on every level and with the infinite possibilities brought about by free will, each copy of ourselves will experience a slightly different version of our life, depending on the infinite choices that we and others make on each level and also the infinite possibilities caused by nature itself.

Although each and every dimension is a cloned copy of the other, variations are endlessly occurring caused by the infinite possibilities of nature and the universe itself, and because of free will, which allows the finite living forms, including us, that exist simultaneously on every dimension to make infinite choices throughout each lifetime.

Every possibility that ever has or ever will be continues to exist in this multi-dimensional universe. Just like the television and radio waves that we broadcast out into space, they go on forever.

If we imagine looking back at the multi-dimensions, simultaneously it's the time of creation, the Big Bang is occurring, the solar system and the earth are evolving, the dinosaurs still roam the earth, the world wars are in progress, man is landing on the moon - also, if we imagine looking linearly ahead of us, mankind has already permanently inhabited the moon, mars and explored the worlds outside our solar system.

All the history of the universe, past, present and future is indelibly recorded in this multi-dimensional universe. Consequently, for you personally, on one level or another, you are yet to be born, you are born, you are growing up, maturing, aging, your life has ended and you are deceased. There are also levels where you never existed at all.

In reality, you are living out every possible variation of your life. Apart from the one life you are aware of, you are also living out the lifetimes of every other decision or choice that you ever have or ever will make, from the important to the mundane.

Plus, you are living out the consequences of the choices of others, both so called good and bad. All those variations of yourself are right here with you right now, experiencing a multi-life that ranges from slightly different to completely foreign to the one you are aware of living.

Although you, or to be more precise, your ego, is having only one experience of your life, your soul, or true self is spiritually connected multi-dimensionally and is experiencing all the infinite versions of your life in all its magnificent variety.

While living out our lives in this multi-dimensional universe with its infinite possibilities, in all dimensions, including this one, we are living out versions of our life which include events that we have no control over, sickness and accidents, natural disasters etc. Here, where our ego consciousness resides, we may survive those incidences virtually unscathed and think ourselves lucky to be alive.

But simultaneously, in other dimensions, we will not survive - in yet others, we will suffer extreme sickness and pain, life threatening injuries and such like. This life experience is also reversed and we may suffer or perish here on this level whilst escaping harm on other levels.

Another traumatic experience is the loss of someone dear to us. These events occur in all dimensions, but when the death of a loved one occurs in this dimension affecting us personally, it may cause us deep sorrow.

Be reassured at these times, your loved one carries on living in infinite other dimensions. When any death occurs, the ego consciousness instantly slips to another dimension where life carries on, so they will not even be aware that in this dimension they have perished. This is also true for ourselves; we have died many, many times during our present life experience.

Although we are unconscious of our total life experience, a tiny shred of reality sometimes filters through to our subconscious, so we can at times become intuitively aware of some of the other experiences in our infinite variety of life.

When a small piece of that knowledge filters through into our conscious mind, strange memories or visions occur and sometimes out of body experiences such as an awareness of floating above our body. In this case, we may be very ill in this dimension, hovering close to death.

On other dimensions, we have most probably died as a result, and those images and emotions have inadvertently filtered through to this dimension where we actually survive that trauma. In these instances a window has momentarily opened into our total reality and we are given a small glimpse of other dimensions where we also exist.

Smaller, less dramatic memories and feelings that crop up in our lifetime occasionally we call déjà vu. In reality though, our whole existence is déjà vu.

Every human being lives a full life. Our mission, while we are here, is to experience every aspect of physical life, and that takes a full life term commitment. The average time it takes to accomplished this today appears to be around seventy five to eighty years or so, although if our mission is still not complete by that age, a few of us may live longer than that.

Although we may 'die' many times in different dimensional levels during our full lifetime term, no one's physical life actually ends until the time is right, and only we can decide that time. How can that be? People die of all ages, babies die, young people die; we can die at any moment.

Remember a very important point in this story - our 'little ego me awareness' is restricted to and thus aware of, only one small, narrow, dimensional level of our full life experience on an infinite number of three dimensional levels in the multi-universe.

When somebody 'dies', they only die on one level. If it so happens to be on this level where your ego consciousness also resides, then you will mourn their death if they are near and dear to you, but the person who 'dies' on this level themselves, (their ego awareness of self) carries on, their ego consciousness instantly switches to another dimension where they continue to survive. To them, their death did not occur.

On the levels where they continue to exist (on which you also exist), you will not be mourning them for they are still alive. If a person is involved in a traffic accident say, simultaneously, in every dimension including this one, all variations of that trauma will be experienced, from death to permanent disabilities, to life threatening wounds, to only suffering a few broken bones.

If on this level, as a result of that accident, that person has a near miss and survives unscathed, we will be patting them on the back, saying, 'You lucky bugger, go buy a lottery ticket' rather than mourning them. Although we all die many times on many dimensional levels, we must live for the full life term – in one dimension or another.

When a baby is born prematurely, or with a defect or disease - on all dimensional levels, you and they will experience the infinite possible variations of their disability, including premature death. If it is your child, that is very difficult to come to terms with.

It needs to be remembered that in this multi-dimensional universe, if your child or loved one dies, causing you to grieve, on other levels they continue to live, grow and mature - and on those levels, you are continuing to love and share in their lives.

It must also be realized that if their disability is cured or lessened to some degree on this level and you are thanking God for being merciful, just remember a sobering thought – on other levels, you continue to tend to a sick child or at worst, you are mourning their death.

On rare occasions, a child may be born only to complete one or two missions, so will be here for a shorter duration than normal. In these special and specific circumstances, they may die young when their missions have been successfully completed.

These children may suffer from such ailments as Senescence, (premature aging) Multiple sclerosis, Cerebral palsy or a host of other illnesses. One attribute they all seem to have in common though is that they appear to know that they may die early and most do not fear their own death. Maybe you know children like that.

Our suffering is appeased if we realize that a child's death has only occurred to allow us, on this level to experience and learn from that emotional trauma. On other levels, they continue to live, with different degrees of that disability, so they can continue to learn and experience, whilst they continue to love and interact with you.

We have all died many times in this lifetime, as we live in an environment of risk, disease and physical danger, but we are completely unaware of that fact, for our ego consciousness simply switches to another level where we remain alive and well. We have no option but to live out a full life.

What's the use of worrying, it never was worthwhile? - goes the old song. You are just one of the many versions of your total self. Whatever you choose to do in life, whatever path you decide to take, there is another version of you living out, not only the opposites, but every other choice you could ever possibly make in life.

Whatever is, let it be, you are spiritually connected to your totality, you can't do wrong. All alternatives are covered. There is no right way or wrong way, there is only life experience - and you have or will experience all the positives and all the negatives in the infinite variety of human life - on one level or another.

For instance, you may decide to move to another city, state or country. On this level you may choose to move to A rather than B and this will be your life experience, but on another level you will choose to move to B instead of A and this will be your life experience on that level.

You may decide to get a job rather than go on to college, become a doctor rather than a bricklayer. You may decide to marry this person instead of that person. No matter what choice you make in life or who you marry or not marry, you will live out all the alternatives on other levels each and every time you make a decision in life.

All those infinite variations of your life are experienced collectively by your soul, although you, your limited, ego consciousness, is only aware of the life resulting from the choices you make on this one level.

There are an infinite number of variations of you on every level of this multi-universe, all with a separate, though spiritually connected ego consciousness, that is each restricted to and thus aware of only one version of your total life experience.

By realizing that it is your soul that is in control and you, your ego consciousness (the person you think you are) is only one of an infinite number of small, fairly insignificant aspects of your total life experience, allows you to not take it all too seriously.

Mankind is under the false assumption that we are special somehow - God's favourite - but we do not take preference over any other living creature at all. Yes, we play an important role in the overall evolution of life - but so does every other life form. Being blessed with the greater intelligence, we are held responsible for ensuring the successful continuation of all life in our little corner of the multi-universe.

Other living creatures great and small fill just as an important slot in the totality of life and all life switches from one dimensional level to another the same as we do, as they experience their own version of the infinite variety of life. When you swat a fly or squash a bug or an insect, they only die on this level, while continuing their life on others.

Animals we slaughter and eat for food, also only die on this level. Omnivores like us need meat to supplement our diet for survival and these animals are legitimately provided to service that need on this level - whilst continuing their life experience on others.

Plants are living creatures too, so although they are also consumed as nourishment for other life forms, including us, on one level or another, they continue to flourish on yet other levels, for they too, must fulfil their destiny of a total life term.

That is not to say that we have a license to indiscriminately kill squash or step on any living creature for the sake of it. Killing an animal (or a plant) for food, or controlling pests if they jeopardize the welfare of another species, is vastly different from killing some living creature, including our own kind just for the sheer pleasure of it.

From mankind down to bacteria, we are all inextricably interwoven into this magnificently diverse multi-universe. Each and every living organism plays a crucial role in the ongoing evolution of life as a whole. All of us creatures, great and small, complement and interact with each other in this wonderfully diverse multi-universe

Explaining how the multi-universe works can only be done in dualistic terms (something here and something else over there) for our life experience is as individual life forms separated in time and space, so any description of life that differs from what we conceive to be our normal, natural state of being must be attempted using a dualistic framework of words and concepts.

The problem is the multi-universe is non-dualistic. It does not consist of different forms separated in time and space. It didn't have a beginning and it won't have an end. It is infinite. It always has been and always will be. To understand the concept of a multi-universe even a little, we are restricted to imagining it as being individual bits and pieces scattered about in space – which in reality, it is not.

We are connected to all dimensional levels by a seemingly separate ego consciousness and our ego consciousness - which is what we recognize as being our individuality - that exists separately on each level, when put together makes up our 'collective ego awareness' which switches from one level to another from moment to moment throughout our lifetime, depending on the choices we make and more specifically, on the beliefs that we hold.

If you believe that life consists of heartache, danger etc, your ego consciousness will gravitate to a level where this appears true. Conversely, if you believe the world is friendly and easy going most of the time, then that's a level your ego consciousness will gravitate towards. In other words, whatever you believe the world to be like, there are dimensional levels that will accommodate your beliefs – and as your beliefs change, so does the level that your ego consciousness will occupy.

It's difficult enough to understand that when we die on one level, our ego awareness instantly switches to another, but because we are so close to ourselves, it is even harder to understand that we are switching levels from moment to moment throughout our lifetime, at the whim of our ever changing choices and beliefs. This constant switching is necessary, as our beliefs and choices change with experience, so that the universe can continually provide us with a full panorama of what life has to offer.

When you look up at the night sky, passed the Milky Way into the space beyond, you are looking at infinity – it has no beginning, no end, it goes on forever. When you concentrate on the stars of the Milky Way itself, plus the moon, the trees and the mountains silhouetted against the night sky, you are looking at the finite contents of that infinite space.

These finite forms appear separate from each other and are of different shapes and sizes. Being finite, they all deteriorate over time, so unlike the infinite space in which they appear, they had a beginning and one day their existence will end.

As the physical observer of this night time spectacle, realize that you are also a finite part of the contents of this infinite space, so you too had a beginning and over time, you will deteriorate and eventually your existence will end.

All finite forms within this infinite space are not real, it's only an illusion. They, and you are there one minute and gone the next. In reality there is only the infinite, eternal nothingness. The world you are experiencing is in reality, the infinite space within your own mind.

There is no duality, no multi-universe, and no separateness, no others, there is just the illusion. Your soul is the one who is experiencing this illusion of life. It accomplishes this by means of an infinite number of life experiences, one for each dimensional level that your collective ego awareness concurrently inhabits – and it's the same story for all other living forms.

The person you think you are is only one of your many illusory selves that are each experiencing one aspect of your total life's journey. In other words, the person you think you are is only a very small part of your total life experience. It is only your soul that experiences your totality by means of your collective ego awareness.

While your life's journey maybe finite, your reality is as infinite as the space beyond, and whilst ever you are here living a life on earth, you will remain oblivious to that fact – and that is how it should be.

Timelessness is a concept we find difficult to comprehend. Everything for us takes time. From the span of a lifetime, to the length of a day, there is a space, a time interval between the beginning and the end. And yet in reality, there may well be no time or space at all. The universe and everything in it could all be contained within an infinite, timeless, spaceless moment.

Trying to imagine the span of time from the Big Bang to the present moment, with all the myriad lifetimes of all the living creatures that have ever inhabited it existing within an Infinite Moment is unbelievably mind boggling. But there is a way we may be able to better understand the concept – and that's by looking at a micro-chip.

Micro-technology is now used to run our world and every day we all access information on the internet for both business and pleasure without even thinking about it. So let's compare the use of a micro-chip in relationship to the Infinite Moment.

If there were say 200 movie stored on a microprocessor that nowadays can be as small as an atom or molecule using nanotechnology, and each movie averaged say 3 hours in length, it would take us around 600 hours, or 25 days straight without a break to watch them all (and that's without any commercials – HA, impossible!).

Each movie might be a story that spans a person's lifetime or maybe many lifetimes and we would feel and experience that time element as we became more engrossed in the story - and yet the total length of time that is included in all those movies put together, fits on one teeny-weeny micro-chip.

Micro-chip technology is for us, quite understandable - and yet we can't get our head around the concept that the seemingly infinitely large universe, with its entire history from go to whoa and all the matter it contains fits in a timeless, spaceless Infinite Moment.

Unlike the microchip, which still has dimensions, even though they may be miniscule, an Infinite Moment would have no dimensions at all and take up no time or space, so in our three dimensional understanding of things, it would be impossible for it to exist –and yet, does it?

Our life's journey is played out concurrently on an infinite number of dimensional levels in the multi-universe, with each level inhabited by a separate ego consciousness of self - which together makes up our collective ego awareness. Why is that so, wouldn't the one ego be sufficient as we only have one soul?

No! Our life experience on each level is different, depending on the choices we make and the ever changing beliefs that we harbour. These multiple egos allow our soul to have separate experiences of our one single life's journey, reacting to the myriad life situations resulting from the multiple choices that are presented to us in any given moment.

This allows for an infinitely variable experience of life. On all levels, our name is the same and our physical body begins the same, and then changes slightly on different levels over time only as a direct result of the life choices that are played out on each of those levels. Every variation of our life is experienced according to those different choices and the various paths we may then decide, albeit unconsciously, to follow.

When we fully realize that our life is much more than we *'think'* it is, we still may live our life exactly as we do now; except we will *'know'* that we are much greater than the part we are playing. Also, we won't take life as seriously as we do now, for we will also *'know'* that we are constantly switching from one level to another, ensuring that we always live out a full life term – and that our loved ones are doing the same.

Everything that exists in this multi-universe is an expression of a boundless, life-giving force, which to our separate ego consciousness is indescribable and unknowable. Anything we try to *'think about'* with regard to this is, by definition, less than it.

Who we truly are is infinite and eternal; we have no boundaries at all. Comparing the person we *'think we are'* to the boundlessness of our true reality is like comparing the width of a human hair to the dimensions of our Milky Way Galaxy.

❝It is not your job to transform the world for others; it is your job to transform the world for you.❞

THE NAKED TABOO

BLAMING others for our problems and limitations is endemic to our society, but society is only made up of people, and we are all people, so logically, society must be us. Society then is not really to blame; we are to blame and the sooner we can become aware of that fact, stop passing the buck onto someone else for our woes and start taking responsibility for our own lives the better.

Society is a drain on our personal freedom and mental growth, yet we are so entrenched in the quagmire of its rules and regulations that it's becoming very difficult to live life without it. We have truly stuffed up our lives by passing on the responsibility for our appearance and behaviour to others, who know no more about life and the way it should be live than we do.

In 'The Naked Taboo' we will see that we are highly regulated in what we are allowed to say, do, wear and behave in the outside world. Society originally came about due to the primitive nature and ignorance of our species. Rules were essential then if we were to survive and protect ourselves from each other.

We have since outgrown this need physically, but mentally we have not in fact we remain inwardly, primitive animals. Imagine for a moment what would happen if a cataclysmic event occurred, a meteor, comet say, and hit the earth causing mass destruction of life. Human survivors would immediately revert back to the savagery that lies dormant just below our skin.

We may believe we are more civilized than that, but even if the few of us were, the mob majority would soon rape, pillage and murder us all, leaving only them to self destruct. Before the chance of that happening occurs, we need to outgrow our need to obey the dictates of society and become mentally self proficient.

If we can do that, society's rules and regulations as they are, will as a consequence become obsolete, for each one of us will become responsible and mature enough to take charge of our own lives, no matter what happens out there in the world, plus we will be ensuring the survival and onward evolution of our species.

I began to look seriously at this dilemma some time back when I needed to attend a doctor's surgery.

There the receptionists and attending nurses were all dressed in smart blue blouse, sleek black slacks, worn over shiny patent leather shoes. They marched about the doctor's surgery like shepherds conscientiously tending their flock of ailing sheep. Their cheerful faces were enhanced by a light and delicate dusting of makeup and a neat smear of lipstick accentuated their smiling lips.

An invisible trail of sweet smelling perfume wafted from their delicate bodies as they authoritatively strutted around the surgery. The reception cum waiting room was like most other doctor's surgery's, arranged so the nurses could keep a motherly eye on the waiting patients, but it also allowed the patients to watch the hustle and bustle of the competent female staff as they went busily about their duties.

I was never one for going to the doctor, but I was impelled to go for a check up on a lung problem. Back when I was young, like a lot of kids my age, I took up smoking. It was thirty years before I had the sense and will power to give up the fags, but unbeknownst to me, the damage had been done.

That was over twenty years ago and I had naively believed I had been lucky enough to have escaped any long term damage, but I was wrong. In the last ten years or so, my love of sucking on those addictive cancer sticks has come back to bite me - but that's beside the point – as I was waiting for the doc I had time to really look at the people and the situation that surrounded me.

I got to thinking, what if we were all naked? Not in a lewd sense, but realistically. Would the staff still go about what they were doing with the same airs and graces, dignity and confidence, or would their whole demeanour change?

Of course this could never happen - and if it did we all know what society's laws would do about it don't we? The place would be swarming with cops, while official looking officials pranced about tut tutting to each other like they were important and knew what they were doing. Yes our society certainly does rule.

Almost everyone in the waiting room was hiding behind a screen of fabric, paint and perfume. A real person was nowhere to be seen. Why? We weren't like that at the beginning when we lived in caves.

Clothing then was mainly animal skins, worn for protection against weather extremes, not to hide our bodies. Why have we gone backwards mentally since those days instead of forward?

When did we decide that a naked body needed to be hidden, something only to be seen by our nearest and dearest – and rarely even then? Was it embarrassment, shame, lust? Why has western society especially, become so perverted, regarding the human body as a sexual object to be coveted and ogled? Why hasn't all human beings done the same?

There are only two models after all; we have either one or the other. Male parts are much the same as any other male's parts and a woman's body is much the same too, except for a few slight differences here and there. What is the need for our bodies to be hidden from view?

Things are different for indigenous people of many countries. In the tropical climates, the men and women are mostly scantily clad. Women think nothing of bearing their boobs and bums to the world; men also are quite happy swinging their body bits in the breeze. It's not shameful for them, there's no leering and drooling at the mouth because someone's naked, it's their normal every day way of life.

They cover themselves, yes - for comfort and protection from the elements – not for vanity. Not for shame or fear of being sexually molested or raped. They are free! Regrettably, we of the 'civilized world' are not free. We are bound up in swaddling cloth and antiquated laws.

Whether we walk around clothed or unclothed is not the point. The point is that we have no option but to hide our bodies in public. We are robots living each day on automatic pilot; following society's antiquated rules and laws that were made long ago. With our present day mindset, we are unable both lawfully and mentally to go about our public business unclothed, for we would be self consciously ashamed – and others would ogle.

Clothes are not the only covering that we hide behind; it's also the cosmetics we plaster all over ourselves. No one can see who we really are, they only see a clown face, a mask that is shown to the outside world. Women now tend to do this more than men, but in times past, it was the men who were done up like prize peacocks.

A lot of us won't show ourselves to the outside world – except to our nearest and dearest, and sometimes not even then – unless we are *'made up'*. Look at the women in the public spotlight - our film stars. Most of them would not be seen dead without a covering of paint and plaster to hide behind. Yet when they are caught on camera by the paparazzi without it, they look like normal, natural, beautiful human beings.

Not all of us are like this of course, there is a heck of a lot that don't wear makeup at all – or very little. That doesn't seem to be a handicap. We also hide our natural human odours behind a curtain of deodorants, perfumes and scents. Why? Do we smell so bad au natural that we fear being burnt at the stake if anyone caught a whiff of what we really smelt like?

There is nothing wrong with wearing makeup perfume and deodorants if we choose to do so. It is only when we have to be *'made up'* before being able to face the outside world that it becomes a problem. Are we so ashamed of how we look and smell that we need to camouflage ourselves so no one will see how ugly and smelly we think we are?

Within our own families, most of us don't cover ourselves up with all that paint and perfume. Our loved ones don't turn up their noses in disgust at our facial features or bodily shape –or the way we smell. Why do we feel the need to present a false image of ourselves to a mob of strangers and casual acquaintances?

During an average day, most of us will unconsciously play many different roles depending on whose company we are in. We tend to act the way we believe other people expect us to act – and of course – vice versa. It is a rare human being indeed, who can remain independent and act naturally without being influenced by others.

The only time that our true personality has a chance of showing itself is when we are alone, and even then – for some of us - self loathing and dislike for our body can be so overbearing that we cannot for example, stand to look at our reflection in the mirror without wearing a covering of paint… For some of us, even that is not enough.

One example is a man in his 50's, who once admitted that in all the years he had been shaving, he never once was able to look at himself eye to eye in the mirror. He had to look askance while lathering his stubble. When asked why, he screwed up his nose in disgust and said he did not like himself and the way he looked sickened him.

In the UK, the Daily Mail reported that around one third of women will not step outside their house without putting some war paint on first – even if they're only going shopping for groceries. Six out of ten wouldn't consider going to work without it – and almost half of all women say they prefer wearing cosmetics than going bare-faced.

For some, it's no different even when they're at home. One in ten of those polled admitted they would never let their partner see them without a full face on. For many women; putting their make-up on is an important part of their day and the thought of people seeing them without it can be horrifying.

The poll also found that the wearing of cosmetics is not really about vanity. Cosmetics are seen as an essential. It's about giving a woman confidence to succeed in every area of their life. This certainly seems to be the case for working women, who are convinced going without make-up, would damage their career prospects.

Cosmetics help us to cover up the truth of who we really are by hiding our bare faces in public. Because of this, make-up has become an essential accessory in any woman's handbag, especially in western society. Almost one in four women in the workforce believes that if they were not 'made up' they would be ignored for a promotion and 37 per cent believe management would assume they didn't take care of themselves.

A professional life coach explained that a reliance on cosmetics can mean a woman is hiding more than a pale complexion or dark circles. "If the reason for wearing make-up lies in the woman feeling worried that people will judge her for the way she looks rather than who she is, that's a problem that needs to be addressed."

Make-up can help with a sense of self-respect. The reality is that we do judge people by how they look and this can be especially important for women in business who often need to appear professional. Women certainly credit their lipstick and mascara for a great deal.

While at home, more than a third of the 3,000 women polled were convinced their husbands would not have been attracted to them had they not been wearing make-up when they met - and even as the relationship progresses, they're not convinced that natural beauty is enough.

The average woman waits at least two-and-a-half months in a relationship before revealing her face without the mask and 14 per cent even went as far as to say they get up early to put their face on before their partner wakes up. Add to that the startling fact that a surprising amount of married couples have never seen each other naked.

What would our world be like if we had no taboos or inhibitions about our bodies? If we were satisfied with the way we naturally looked and smelled? How would our attitudes to life and each other change? Would we be more relaxed with our body and those of others? Hiding our real selves in public is well and truly entrenched in our western society. It's too late to change the rules or people's attitudes - so maybe it's a change of mind that is needed.

A different culture, (the customary beliefs of a religious, social or racial group) who's attitudes and values, devised by the leaders of those groups, is the real culprit. A culture that controls a society is not really a bad thing except that it is run by human beings. In its broadest sense, the particular culture we each belong to is the culprit that has placed restrictions and taboos on how we appear and behave when in the public eye.

The requirement to cover up our body in public, the countless behavioural laws that we must follow, that have now become ingrained into the way we live our life, all stem from society's dictates, accumulated over time by the few humans who in their ignorance and imagined superiority, decide how we all should live – and die.

Society is a collection of governments, organizations and committees that, amongst other things, attempt to control problems such as, corruption, greed and violence. The only problem with that is, the controllers – the law makers, the deciders on what is best for everyone else are themselves just as corrupt, greedy and violent– or maybe more so as their decisions are influenced by their own narcissist needs.

Once they make sure that they are okay, they may then enact laws and conditions that seem fair to all, but are they? Look at our politician's salaries and perks for instance. Our leaders and law makers are adept at making elaborate excuses for feathering their own nest first.

The banking industry imposes high interest rates on loans and any other service they provide, far above what may be deemed fair. The meagre interest rates that we can earn on our own savings are governed by the banks forecasted profit margins, exorbitant executive salaries and high dividends doled out to their many, greedy shareholders.

The insurance industry (which really is a protection racket that's been legalized) is high up in the greedy stakes. They make us pay through the nose for protection, only to deny compensation on some spurious technicality in time of need. Our leaders, who control so much of our lives, would rate together as the greediest and most corrupt culprits of all.

The fashion industry is included amongst 'the culprits that control our lives' where the self proclaimed fashionable few decide for the rest of us what to wear and what not to wear - what is in fashion today and what is no-wear tomorrow. If we are gullible enough and follow their ever changing fashion whims, then we will be forever changing our wardrobe.

Another big problem we have today is with the euthanasia debate. The problem is not in actually deciding to take our own life if we feel the quality has declined into too much pain and suffering, but without consideration of our feelings, others in society, pompously believing that they know better than we do; unsympathetically impose blanket laws against it.

It's our life after all. We are the ones suffering the pain, not them. But we are forced to choose between years of distress or breaking society's law. We can't be penalized of course if we do end our life, but the authorities are very sneaky and threaten to penalize our loved ones and helpers if we do. The threat of imprisonment for anyone who assists us prevents us from making that decision.

The imagined threat of legalizing euthanasia is that some people will try and take the easy way out and consider suicide – and that may occur, but this cannot be stopped or controlled by imposing an all encompassing law against euthanasia. Rather, it is better mediated with common sense, awareness and intelligent consultation.

There is nothing inherently wrong with receiving advice from others if we then have the option to take it in and best decide for ourselves how we conduct our life - without penalty, but when it becomes a law, when others decide for us while we have little or no say in the matter, and then we have a problem.

If we don't conform, we, or our loved ones in the case of euthanasia, are penalized and/or imprisoned, which as we know, certainly isn't the solution – and yet, this is what we repeatedly do. To leave the conduct of our lives up to the determination of others, who believe they know better than we do, is something we must all outgrow.

Societies came about because we are social animals, we like to congregate. That is an instinctive function of our human nature, but because of our mental immaturity, over hundreds of years, society's rules, laws and taboos have run amok. In an attempt to find solutions, lawmakers, governments, committees, organizations, tend to seek an outside authority such as someone that is believed to be more intelligent than the average Joe.

We consult sociologists, psychologists, psychiatrists, religious leaders, any so called expert who we believe can supply the answers to the problems we have, but instead of resolving them, they create laws (or taboos) against, fines and jail terms for, law enforcement agencies to protect, penalties to deter, incentives to obey, rehabilitation centres to help - which are all useless measures, for as is evident, the problems we have not only persist, but escalates over time.

No matter how much thought is put into it and how earnest we may be to find a solution to our over-regulated lives, we are only treating the symptoms. We, and the so called experts, can only look at what has happened before to try and get answers - and the answers are simply not there.

What has happened has happened already. If there was a solution there, there would not now be a problem to deal with. Social media only adds to our woes by publicizing our immaturity worldwide. New problems need new solutions. New solutions cannot be found in what has already occurred. Any problems we have with society, no matter what they are, need a new approach.

All of our major advances, all of the ways we have found to solve or alleviate any of our problems in the past has been caused by a flash of inspiration, a sudden conscious seeing of the problem, which holds within it, the solution. Not from governmental committees, discussion groups, law makers etc, sitting around banging their heads together in their so called wisdom, then deciding on our behalf, how it might be solved.

The Naked Taboo isn't about proving that society's rules, laws and taboos are right or wrong, what it is attempting to show is that we all follow those rules, laws and taboos unconsciously. We are unaware that every day of our lives we constantly and robotically obey the dictates that our society has laid down in the ancient past, which has become deeply rooted in our everyday mentality.

We automatically follow practices set down many long years ago, practices that have been fiddled with over and over again but never changed. We are living by the same code of conduct that our distant ancestors lived by. Society's rules, laws and taboos have become old, tired and outdated, they desperately need to be changed - but before that can happen, we must firstly become aware that we are blindly following them.

The woman at the mirror putting on makeup is not 'there' in her mind. She is elsewhere, maybe remembering what happened earlier or anticipating what may happen later. The same goes when we do anything - After our shower say, we dry ourselves, apply the deodorant, the perfume, the antiperspirant, but we do it all unconsciously.

Millions of us all over the world commute to work and back each weekday to conduct our business, making sometimes very important decisions, all on automatic pilot. We are not present, so we are unable to decide whether we need to continue doing whatever we are doing in the same way or not – or that we even need to do it at all.

Because we are lost in reverie most of the time, our important decisions are compromised, which is what our governments, community leaders and law makers are doing all the time. How can we effectively change what needs to be changed when our minds are not there, instead we are lost in an antiquated mentality of a time long gone?

By becoming aware of the way we are living our life every moment, society's rules, laws and taboos will automatically change for the better. The obsolete will be deleted, the outdated will be updated and the very few that are still relevant today will be kept as they are, making life for us all much less complicated and our minds much more evolved.

Governments, who represent us and act on our behalf, are made up of an unruly mob of rowdy politicians who spend most of their time squabbling and bickering amongst themselves across their parliamentary floors while at the same time enacting laws and imposing taxes that affect us all in a vain attempt to plug up the never ending holes in society's flimsy framework.

Religious institutions of all denominations create laws and taboos in an attempt to control and convert us to *their* particular belief system, sometimes ostracizing or persecuting us if we don't comply. As an aside, they also greedily take money and property from their congregations, so as to build up their own church coffers, strengthening their stranglehold on the gullible.

Wars have been waged since day dot in an attempt to get what someone else has, oil, water, land, food, empires etc, or to control, subdue, convert or annihilate others simply because their skin is a different colour or their beliefs are different, or they simply believe they are inferior to them in some way.

Dictators and despots persecute their countrymen using murder and torture as a weapon in an attempt to control them. People, who are suffering under such a dictatorship, eventually get sick and tired of being suppressed and in protest, riot throughout their country in an attempt to get rid of their suppressers.

Protesters march the streets of every town and city worldwide waving their placards, complaining and demonstrating against others whom they believe are the cause for what is wrong in their life, in an attempt to change governments and authorities into complying with what they believe is right.

Unions strike or go slow for a better pay packet or better working conditions or some other gripe against those they believe have caused them to be hard done by. They rally against their companies, their bosses, their governments, blaming them for their troubles instead of themselves.

On and on it goes in a never ending, unwinnable cycle of blaming someone else instead of realizing that we are ourselves to blame. While ever we believe that others are at fault and that they need to be controlled or coerced into thinking the same as we do, we will remain stuck in a 'Them versus Us' dark age mentality while our society's taboos will continue to be obeyed without question at all times. What is mankind doing to himself?

"Beauty is embedded in everything, but everything is embedded in us."

BEING HUMAN

Regardless of what others may say, if they are here, they're living in the belief they are their physical body and name - their ego. They might profess to be egoless, enlightened, consciously aware, a guru, a mystic, Jesus, Buddha, whatever their claim, while we can see them and interact with them, they are on the same level as us. They regard themselves as we do, an entity separate from everything and everyone else.

Anyone who has advanced enough to conquer the ego's domination over their life would simply not be here. There would be no need; the world we live in is the ego's exclusive domain. There is a cosmic law: You can only interact with those who are either on the same level as you - or just slightly below. The ones that have progressed would have moved upward mentally - out of the range of our awareness.

Thankfully, we're becoming aware of who we really are, including the realization that our ego is only a small part of our true nature and that up to this stage of our evolution it has messed up and complicated so much of our daily life. We are now though on the threshold of a major evolutionary leap in which we will either sink or swim.

Who we think we are is in the past. We are living out our lives primarily from memories of what was, not from life as it is happening now. It is time to change that. If we learn to swim, we will progress to the next stage of our evolution. If we sink, then it's back to square one and we start all over again from scratch (as we have probably done many times before) and then see if the next time, we can learn to swim.

Cosmically speaking it doesn't matter a damn how long it takes or if we succeed or fail. After all, we have all of eternity in which to learn. But to us as a human species, it does. There is something within us that wants to succeed. We need to become consciously aware of our emotions, feelings, beliefs, judgments etc, so we can raise them up from their unconscious, robotic like, reactionary level, which is our normal approach. Some of these are:

MEMORY:

If we believe we are our ego, we live in the past, simple as that. Most of us don't know what we are doing right now in the present moment, and if we don't know that, we don't know anything - and that's the problem. Life is passing us by. Our thoughts are living our life. If we are walking down the street say, we are thinking about something else other than us walking down the street.

One of our major hang-ups is that we are compelled by our ego to put a label on everything and everyone. We then place those tagged images in memory for future reference. That's quite okay, we need to remember certain things to physically survive, but this has taken us over, so before we can recognize anything at all we must firstly refer to similar events from the past.

We begin to accumulate a record of every life experience from the time we are born and the longer we live, the greater our store of records grows. Apart from the basic survival memories, we unnecessarily continue to accumulate images, eventually becoming lost in a pile of stale, outdated records of events in our past that serve no real purpose.

FEAR:

Even though most of us would not admit it, fear is always there in the back of our mind. We fear anything that may endanger our well being - fear of loss, fear of death, fear of being hurt, and we will take appropriate action to try and avoid such risks. While ever we believe we are our body, name and ego, then that is the way we must live our lives.

Even the so called happy go lucky people are not as happy as they make out. They have that same uneasiness within. Whenever a crisis occurs, or when things go wrong, they lose their cool, their happy demeanour is replaced by anxiety and fear. All this is subconscious of course but nevertheless, it is the normal way we approach our daily lives.

We are afraid of being hurt, of not getting the most out of life, of not rising up to our fullest potential, of not having enough money or possessions. We are afraid of pain, death, loneliness, of losing the securities we have. We are afraid that the pleasures we have will no longer be available tomorrow. We are also afraid our loved ones won't love us, and we are even more afraid that we won't love them.

We live in fear. We try to make it go away. But fear is all powerful; it is constantly there within our minds. We try to forget it - pretend it doesn't exist, but it's always there. It influences the majority of our life experience. Most of us will reject the assumption that we are a fearful person, but if we can become consciously aware of how fearful we really are, it will be the first step in eradicating fear from our lives.

LONELINESS:

If we did not want anything from life there would be no fear. Simple as that! The only reason that we are afraid is that we want someone or something that we don't have - or have and don't want to lose. This includes the desire to continue to have our self, the person we think we are, our body, our mind, our personality, us.

There are people in our life that love us and we love them, that's natural to most of us. Sounds great, but underneath, we are always afraid of losing that love. We are afraid that they might stop loving us, so we compromise. Unconsciously, we act and react when we are with them in such ways so as to ensure that their love for us will continue.

We are not being honest with ourselves or them, because if we were, we think we might jeopardize our relationship with them. Even if everything is going well, there is always the fear that they might to die and we'll lose them that way. This causes us even more fear because we are helpless to do anything about it.

Our want is to live forever for we are afraid of the uncertainty of death, or to be more precise, the loneliness of not being anymore. Loneliness is entirely different than being alone, which is really being contented with oneself, a quiet satisfaction with our own company, a state of desiring nothing from life.

To suffer from loneliness means we continually want the company of someone else or something else. We always need to be in a crowd, or to be occupied. The more we fear loneliness, the more people and things we will attempt to accumulate around us to block that fear.

We believe that by having that something or someone else, our mind will be preoccupied with people and objects, so we can ignore the fact that in reality, we are always alone within ourselves. To become consciously aware of that, allows us to move forward in our learning process.

BELIEF:

What we believe primarily determines who we think we are and re-enforces our faith that we will continue on forever as a separate individual. Organized religion jumped on this band wagon a long time ago. They preach that if we believe and do what the church tells us, then we will be protected and need not fear death and damnation. If we don't believe or do as they preach, then we may very well be condemned to oblivion.

Whatever mainstream religion promises us, heaven and eternal life, or eternal damnation in hell, it is all playing on our fear of not existing anymore. Even hell with all its supposed fire and brimstone is better to believe in than oblivion, for in hell, we would still continue to exist.

Our belief system is second hand. It began forming when we were born and is mainly made up of the beliefs and opinions of others passed down to us, our parents especially. Aunties, uncles, close friends, school teachers etc have also contributed. As we grow into adulthood, we may vary those beliefs somewhat, but in the main, we retain the same basic set of beliefs formed in early childhood.

What we think of ourselves, how we approach and tackle life's problems, how we see and react to the world in general, depends on our belief system. As we experience more of life, our beliefs formed in childhood become ever more rigid and unmovable until they become so covered in the murkiness of the past that they become immune to change.

Usually it takes a major shock, loss or extreme tribulation for us to break free of our ingrained belief system. Then it is usually the case that, not knowing how to handle the situation, our true self then has a chance to shine through into our consciousness, giving us the opportunity to learn what life is trying to teach us.

NEED:

Inextricably woven into our belief system is the insatiable need for more. Even people who appear to be 'well off' still crave even more riches, more money, more fame, a bigger and more lavish house, car, lifestyle etc. The amount of wealth, possessions or social status they have will make little difference to their opinion that to be more complete as a person, they need more stuff.

Not only individuals suffer from this need for more disease, it is also true for us collectively. Banks, companies, corporations, governments etc. all have that same unquenchable thirst, as we all know. Even if they double, treble or quadruple their yearly profits, their need for greed continues on unabated.

The problem is we identify with having, it is a part of who we think we are, but our satisfaction in having is a relatively shallow and short lived one. Concealed within it remains a deep seated sense of dissatisfaction, of incompleteness, of not enough. 'I don't have enough yet,' by which we really mean, 'I am not enough yet.' and never will be, so the search goes endlessly on and on.

There are needs that are essential for our survival. These are the basic needs for sustenance and shelter. Each one ensures the continuation of our body, for without them, we would not survive. They are the only legitimate and necessary needs.

As for any other needs, they are unnecessary excess baggage in our ongoing quest for pleasure and self gratification. All we are chasing is past memories of what was. They do not exist now. They are dead and gone, remaining only as a remembered pleasure from the past.

The solution to our insatiable need for more is to simply live in the now where there is no *need* for anything at all. There is only peace and contentment in the wholehearted, unconditional acceptance of the uncluttered present moment.

LOVE:

Ordinarily we think of love as a necessity we can't live without – a commodity to acquire and own, to keep and not lose. Everybody seeks love. We are told to love our country, to die for it if necessary. Religion tells us to love God and if we do, we will be rewarded, if we don't, we are threatened with damnation.

We fall in love with someone, if they do the same, well and good, if they don't and dare to love another, we become jealous. Love can then turn to hate. What we think of as love demands something in return. 'If you love me, I'll give you my company, I'll give you sex, I'll compromise myself for you. If you don't, I'll withhold my love until you come to your senses.

When we say we unconditionally love someone, it's actually conditional, for we *do* expect something in return – their love – but what if they don't love us back, and what if they reject our advances? What then? Does our unconditional love for them continue on regardless as it unconditionally should?

Love can never make any demands whatsoever and still be called love. When we say I love you, what we are really after is pleasure, our gratification. We are fearful of losing that love at any moment, for then we would suffer the opposites such as heartache and loss. Love has no opposite. To want to hold onto someone and expect a return is not love at all, but pleasure masquerading as love.

The closest we come to unconditional love as human beings, is our love for our children, especially when they are young. Eventually though, as they grow up and into adulthood, we tend to place certain conditions on that love. 'Behave the way I think you should and I will continue to love you unconditionally. Do something I don't think is good and I won't love you unconditionally quite as much! True Love is unconditional. To be consciously aware that what we call love is really only pleasure is an important step in our lessons in life.

JOY:

Unhappiness is a disease of human beings that is in epidemic proportions. One of the main reasons for that unhappiness is negativity. The state of the world outside, which is full of negativity, reflects like a mirror what we feel inside. Our outside and our inside are exactly the same and it's what is happening inside of us that is the source of our unhappiness, not what is out there.

To see what we are really like inside all we need do is take a look at what is happening out there in the world, the news headlines explains it all. We are all trapped in this web of negativity to some degree.

Happiness is the poor substitute for Joy. Happiness lives in the memories of the past and the anticipated future, 'I think I was happy yesterday and I want to be happy again tomorrow' so I look outside to try and find or keep it. We can never find it out there so the quest for happiness goes endlessly on and on. We may think we have it for a moment, but then something bad happens and we lose it.

We depend entirely on what happens in our life for our happiness – but what do we get if we can't have what we want - if that prized possession or person or achievement that we want so badly is denied? We don't get happiness – instead we get unhappiness, something we try so desperately to avoid.

We don't really understand the fact that *'what happens'* is a very unstable thing. We can never tell with any certainty what will happen at any moment in time and when something does happens, it is not always as we would wish, for it does not rely on our personal desires, but is simply 'what is!'

The joy of being cannot be experienced by having some-thing or person, achievement or event, or through anything that happens. Joy cannot come to us. Joy just is. It emerges from the timeless dimension within us, from consciousness itself. Both Joy and Love is who we really are.

PEACE:

Probably peace is our most misunderstood desire and the one we look for most. There are many ways in which we believe we can attain peace. Most of us would say that a suspension of world hostilities would likely rate as one of the main ways of achieving it. We also believe that peace can be experienced by the elimination of many of our annoyances in daily life.

If our rowdy neighbours would only shut up and stop their arguing, or turn down their music, if the kids would just be quiet for a minute, if the person next door using the leaf blower would drop dead, or if our daily work load wasn't so hectic and so on. We are always at war with something, the war against terrorism - The war against crime and drugs - The war against cancer - The war against poverty etc.

We can never achieve peace by changing anything out there. As with our sense of love and joy, our wish for peace and quiet relies on something happening out there, someone or something must stop upsetting our peace of mind, which is not really peace but a desire that if achieved, will give us pleasure. We need to stop being a seeker of peace and become a finder.

Peace can only be found within us, it will never be found on the outside, with anything happening, or not happening as the case may be, although most of us spend a great deal of our lives vainly searching for it out there. Peace is not a commodity; you can't *have* it for it is not an acquisition or an emotion.

There is no need to search for it for we already have it; we just have to find it within. The degree of peace that we see out there in the big wide world is exactly the same degree of inner peace that we experience. There is no difference because it is our inner self that dictates what the world we see out there is like.

Love, Joy and Peace are our eternal states of being – God in form. They are who we really are. If we can become consciously aware of that fact we will magically change ourselves and if we are able to do that, we will change our world.

SEX:

Procreation is genetically programmed into us to insure the continuation of our species. We don't have that to ourselves of course; it is programmed into every living creature on this planet. Because it is so vital for the continuation of life, we are instinctively attracted to the act of sexual intercourse, where we become enthralled in an intensive and addictive moment in time.

Orgasm itself is timeless, an abandonment, a giving up of oneself for a moment where we are lost in the other person, in the sexual act itself. Even though sex is genetically programmed into us, it is one of the few places, or maybe the only place where we can experience the timeless now moment.

We have never lost the original purpose for our attraction to the opposite sex or the sexual act, which is to reproduce. At the right time, when women ovulate, the instinct to copulate is heightened. This has been hidden to some extent beneath our need for self gratification. For some of us it becomes the focal point of our lives.

Sex becomes so extraordinarily important that we become addicted to it. Most of us think of our sexuality as being only in the genital area and deals only with genital responses. Reproduction then becomes less important and the emphasis switches to self gratification.

We forget that there is a lot more to sexuality, which usually involves another person with separate feelings and needs. We selfishly want them to pander to our wishes and if they don't, we are turned off or get angry or disappointed, creating sexual tension in the process.

We have substituted true love and warmth for sexuality. If we could experience the passion of living in our daily lives, sexuality would not be the problem it is. It would be just something we either do or don't do, depending on its appropriateness at the time.

ANGER:

Everyone of us gets angry to some degree in our lives, it can vary from mild irritation to impatience to intolerance to indignation and finally we can explode into a temper tirade, the sole objective then being to verbally mock, humiliate or possibly even physically abuse the person who has dared to affront us.

This can also be the case for us collectively when our governments and institutions - religious institutions especially - believe they have been wronged. Look at all the religious wars and the violence in the Middle East at the moment, waged simply because one side has a different religious belief than the other side.

Anger is uncompromising, exhibiting uncontrollable feelings of extreme dislike or even hatred. It exudes feelings of self-destructiveness. Anger may provoke feuds that can go on for many years. Any provocation can result in an anger outburst.

For instance, it can be instigated by an individual insinuating blame on another, whether it's warranted or not, or who belittles or spurns their love, or simply does something they don't like. Road rage is a common form of this type of uncontrolled anger. Thankfully most of us are not as volatile as that.

If we look honestly at ourselves, we may see a connection between what we feel when we think we have been unjustly accused or things don't go the way we think they should and the bubbling cauldron of anger that subsequently arises and seethes within us, creating the spontaneous urge to react angrily.

Whenever we get angry we need to become consciously aware of our anger before it erupts and realize that it is ourselves that suffer the most from these outbursts. Self awareness puts a damper on anger's fires. It's impossible for us to be angry now, anger needs time, the past and future in which to brew and percolate, in the present moment there is simply nothing to be angry about. It's quite okay whatever happens.

VIOLENCE:

Human beings are the most violent creatures on earth. That might be a difficult fact to come to terms with, but it's true. Predatory animals may appear to be more violent than us, but they are not. Their violence is the same basic instinct that they started out with and still use today. They use violence to kill and eat to survive.

We used the same instincts for survival at the beginning of our existence as well, but we had a big advantage over the other animals - we developed a more sophisticated brain, which gave us the ability to reason and to learn from our mistakes.

We are an extremely violent animal and an exceptionally successful one. We have casually destroyed entire species around us completely without batting an eyelid and more are dying every day. We have spread our progeny all over the planet to plague proportions and as we do so, other less well equipped species die out.

Our evolutionary advantage is our mind and brain. That is what has made our species the successful animal it is. We have the intelligence, but not the maturity. We no longer need to fight for survival, so we have turned our violent nature upon ourselves and the planet we live on.

We are attempting to destroy our very selves. If we as a species are to continue to evolve, we must come to terms with our violent nature. We are all capable of violence, even if we think we are not. We all get irritable, impatient and frustrated at times, emotions that if provoked can escalate to anger and rage, all of which is violent.

It is high time for us to move on from our early fight or flight instincts that once were vital for our survival, mechanisms we now no longer require. We must evolve or perish. How can we do that, so as to continue to exist and prosper? That is a crucial question that we all must now face and answer.

PRIDE:

Being quietly aware that we are worthy beings, that we are doing the best that we know how, that we are an integral part of this wonderful world, is sometimes called pride, but there is no judgment of others or of ourselves, so that is not really pride in its true meaning - just a quiet appreciation of self and everything else.

There are many different subtle forms of pride. For example, (and we have all done this) we are about to tell someone the news of what happened. "Guess what? You haven't heard yet? Let me tell you". If we are alert enough, we may be able to detect a momentary sense of smug satisfaction within ourselves, a puffing up of pride, just before telling someone the news – even if it's bad news.

It is due to the fact that there is an imbalance in our favour between us and the other person. For a brief moment in time, we know more than them. The satisfaction we feel is pride. Even if the other person is the president or the pope, we feel superior in that moment because we know more than them.

Some people play sport for the sheer enjoyment of it, win or lose – but to some it's war, a matter of pride, a competition that must be won at all costs. If they are not winning, they are apt throw a tantrum and scream obscenities at whomever or whatever impedes them and they usually believe others are at fault, not them. We all know people like that.

What is happening is that they are falling short of the expectations they have put on themselves, how special they think they are, the wins that they have had in the past, in which they take great pride in. This self belief then is projected forward into the future with the prospects of the pride in the wins to come.

Pride is a psychotic disease that needs the past and future in which to develop and can cause all of us to become argumentative or even hostile if our self belief is affronted. Pride cannot exist in the present moment, where there is only a quiet awareness that we are all equally worthy beings.

DECISIONS:

What should we do, where should we go, what do we wear, buy etc, etc? Our deciding what to do or not to do makes up the greater part of our thoughts in our daily lives. Most decisions are mundane choices so when a decision we make is the right one, we take no particular notice of it, in fact our action is robotic and we usually remain completely unaware that we made a decision at all.

If our decision is wrong however, we do take notice and maybe after a lot of swearing and cursing, promise ourselves to try not to make that same mistake again. We regret any wrong decisions we make, especially if in hindsight we believe we would have been better off by deciding differently, consequently we blame ourselves for our own stupidity.

Typical statements at such times might be, 'Why did this have to happen to me?' 'Why did I make that stupid choice?' 'If only I had let things stay as they were!' 'I wish I could have my time over again!' 'How could I have been such a bloody idiot?'

Before we can regret any decision in our life we first have to experience the event that caused us to decide, otherwise we could never have experienced either the satisfaction of making the right decision or the regret of making the wrong decision. Nothing would have happened; therefore we would never have lost, gained or learned anything.

We need to make wrong decisions more than right decisions really, to make our life work. We survived and evolved as a species by making lots of wrong decisions and learning the lessons they held in the process. A wrong decision helps us to learn, for once the lesson is learned, we are less likely to make that same mistake again, allowing us to then make the right decision next time, thus continue to evolve as a human being.

So a wrong decision is really just a right decision in its infancy. It is the wrong decisions we make contrasted against the right decisions that allows us to correct the wrong next time a similar situation crops up, so without a wrong, we cannot have a right.

CHOICE:

Strangely, you'd reckon it would be a good thing to have plenty of choices in life, but is more choices really a good thing? The very need to choose means that there are alternatives, which one should we choose - the right one or the left one - this one or that one – which one?

If we are aware each time we have a choice, we will see that in the need to choose there is inner confusion – a decision has to be made – which one should I choose is a conflicting statement. The conflict arises at the point of choosing and continues afterwards because we can never then know if choosing the other alternative would have been better for us than the choice we made.

The necessity to choose brings about inner disquiet, a decision needs to be made – even between two good alternatives, it makes no difference. Doubt is always one of the results of choice and with doubt in our mind, a peaceful and joyful life is impossible. We will always be wondering if we chose rightly.

We go from one choice to the other trying to resolve our conflicts – our social problems, our political alliances, our wars, our terrorism - but anything done out of conflict only creates more conflict. The evidence is plain to see out there. Whenever any action is done out of conflict, there is always a regret. Our mind plays the 'what ifs' game. To be truly free is to have no choice at all. If we knew what to do there would be no choice.

With clear vision, the need for choice magically disappears. Unconditional acceptance of what is keeps our life on track. The hardest thing of all for any of us is to have the trust to just let go and let our life be lived – that's another lesson of life.

RELATIONSHIPS:

Pleasing relationships appear to be the only relationships that have any value for us, but that is not the case. Unpleasant relationships, whether with problematic people, loud or nasty neighbours, unruly kids, roadragers and such like, or even being caught up in the drama of riots, war and terrorism, hold within those relationships, important lessons we need to learn.

Our conscious awareness of when an unwanted situation arises in our lives presents us with the opportunity to see that a different reaction may bring about a better result rather than the automatic, unconscious and emotional response we habitually use. We are given a choice on each occasion to either learn from that unpleasant relationship or identify with it, thus becoming lost in its emotional turmoil.

This means then, that in our total physical experience, even those uncomfortable interactions, whether learnt or unlearnt form the basis of our ever expanding physical life experience. An unpleasant relationship is no different really, than making a wrong decision in life. We don't like either but we need to experience both of these life situations so as to learn and evolve.

People often believe that the benefits of interacting with others is mostly to do with combining talents and actions in order to accomplish the things that need to be done in a society, but our human relationships are much more important than that.

We are helping one another define our individual and collective selves. In other words, even the briefest of encounters with another person is actually contributing to our overall expansion as a human being, so bad relationships are just as important as our good relationships.

Relationships are important, we need them and they need us for the experiences and the lessons that are held in those encounters. We are all teaching each other as well as learning from each other, every moment of our lives. Our relationship with others, both good and bad, adds immeasurably to our own growth.

We must become keenly aware that that person or persons who is interacting with us in any given moment is there to teach us something – and we are there to teach them something.

INSPIRATION:

Edison's light bulb had nothing to do with a lighted candle. He may have studied a candle at the start but the inspiration to put a filament inside a vacuum flask and heat it with electricity was completely new. It came to him in a flash. This little bit of inspiration solved a problem, taking away the darkness and lighting up our world.

When Fleming discovered penicillin, the solution literally flew in through the window. Penicillin is a type of mould that up until then, was thought to be a dirty residue of rotting or decaying matter. The last thing anyone would think then was that mould could heal – but it did and still does – it was inspirational and a new way of looking at medicine.

Trains, planes and automobiles were all inspired inventions. Our ancestors could have had no possible way of envisioning in their minds, such strange contraptions, for there was nothing on earth to compare them with. They were completely new conceptions!

When thinking about mankind's upcoming voyage to Mars, scientists are trying to plan a spaceship to take us there. Those plans are based on the past – propulsion provided by rockets and such. They have no way of 'thinking' up or picturing some completely new way of propulsion because they can only look at how they did it in the past.

It's a pretty good bet that in the near future, some scientist will have an inspiration, an out of the ball park vision of a completely new way to propel our astronauts into outer space. At the moment, there is no way that any of us can imagine what that way may be. It is something as yet new to our mind and needs inspiration, not thought to discover it.

Of course, once something new is invented or discovered, or a problem solved, it becomes part of the past, so next time we have a similar problem, we are hit with the same old dilemma – until we look at it also in a new way. We can only think old. To solve our problems, we need to be inspired, to see our problems from another angle, completely and clearly, without the handicap of thought.

KNOWLEDGE:

Like all life on earth, we human beings are part of a continuing evolutionary process. On the physical level, we have evolved as we should. Our body and brain have adapted over time to the environment we now live in. Our mentality however, has not. Sure, we have learned a lot of things since our cavemen days. We have improved in leaps and bounds intellectually, but that's not evolution, that's knowledge learned from trial and error.

Humans with the biggest brains lived 20,000 to 30,000 years ago in Europe. Known as Cro-Magnons, they were tall with barrel chests and large jaws and teeth. Most impressive, however, were their brains, with males averaging a volume of 1500 cubic centimetres!

The human brain has since become smaller, now averaging 1350cc, a decrease equivalent in volume to a tennis ball. One scientist remarked that, "We may have smaller brains than early humans but that does not mean we are less intelligent."

There are many assumptions for this decrease in brain size, but it is quite possible that – because we no longer need so much survival information – our brain no longer needs to be so big. Our physical makeup also is making allowances for the fact that it is no longer necessary to be always ready for fight or flight– now it is up to our mental outlook to catch up.

Physical evolution of our species is progressing along nicely; our mental evolution however, is not. We live in a time of great upheaval. There are problems of ecology that involves the fact that we are making the world uninhabitable, the problems of overpopulation, violence, racial tensions, alcohol and other drugs.

But what are we supposed to do? The old unconscious instinct for survival based on violence has been largely in us since mankind took his first steps. Now the time of our adolescence has past and so has unconscious evolution become inadequate if we are to survive!

Knowledge is now not enough. Conscious awareness is urgently needed if we are to continue to evolve – which means we have to wake up and become acutely aware of the detrimental effects we are having on ourselves and our environment.

FORGIVENESS:

When we begin to consciously look at the way our mind works, especially the way we react to people and events in our daily lives, we discover one of the keys to the successful evolution of our mind. We see that if we are not consciously aware of the way we are reacting to life's many challenges, then we have no hope of changing poor reactions for better ones.

Our mind is full of beliefs and judgments that we are completely unaware of. We are like robots most of the time - unconsciously filtering our daily life through a veil of opinions built up from the past and then making an assumption on what we believe life is like.

This means of course, that we are not seeing life as it is, only our perception of life viewed through a curtain of prejudices beliefs and judgments, which as a result makes us very unforgiving. We may not believe that we are an unforgiving person, but by standing aside and watching how we automatically react to incidents in everyday life and our resulting judgments, we will be shocked to find that that is not so.

In our caveman days it was not advisable to forgive anyone, (man or beast) who maybe stole our food, shelter or our women or men, for that could be disastrous to the future of our clan. We needed to not forgive them, so as to guard against them doing it again. But that is not now the case.

Whether we forgive or not is not really the problem so much as the unawareness of the fact that we are unforgiving. Un-forgiveness is a cancer that spreads its tentacles in the unconscious darkness of our mind causing us to critically judge others and life itself. We cannot cure that disease if we are not even aware that we have it.

Un-forgiveness is a relic of the past that, although no longer needed, we still unconsciously hang onto. As with all our other negative emotions, it cannot exist in a conscious mind where there is only unconditional acceptance of what is and forgiveness for every person and event that we encounter in our daily lives. There is no need then to do anything, the conscious seeing of the way we are is the cure to all our mental ills.

IGNORANCE:

Everybody is concerned about the ever growing problem of drugs, so the powers that be are attempting to do something about it in the vain hope of solving this problem. We have outlawed drugs, and built rehabilitation centres etc, but to no avail. The reason being is that we are ignorant of the real problem, the problem with drugs is not the drugs themselves; they are only the symptoms.

If only symptoms are dealt with, when we believe we have solved a problem, it will pop up in some other place. The trouble is that narcotics offer us a more interesting alternative than living life. Taking drugs dulls us to the stresses of daily life and as long as that's the case, there will be a continuing problem with drugs no matter what laws we pass or how great an effort we make to stop the spread of their usage.

Not only drugs are used as a distraction to life, such things as extreme sports, loud music and many other forms of exhilarating diversions are used - the latest being the internet - especially on mobile devices like tablets and smart phones that give us access anywhere we are to social media such as Facebook and Twitter. All of these can be used as ways of occupying our mind and dulling us to life.

Artificial distractions are not a problem in themselves unless we cannot live without them. If we suffer a downer after coming off a high from indulging in any pastime, sport etc, suffering such emotions as depression and boredom until we can experience them again, they are no different to drugs – in fact they are a drug.

Some of us always need something to do, something to take our mind off the humdrum of daily life. Drugs, excitement, entertainment, thrills and spills give us the illusion of an exciting life. Whenever life is peaceful and there are no dramas occurring, boredom, restlessness and irritation set in.

While ever we are ignorant of how we are living our lives, we will continually look in the wrong place to find any meaning for it. If it's the wrong place then, where do we look? For it has become imperative that we find it.

PLEASURE:

Whether we are aware of it or not, we are continually searching for some sort of enjoyment in our life. We want to experience all the high sounding stuff like peace, joy and love, commodities that we believe will help fill the emptiness within, but instead, we mistakenly pursue their poor substitute, pleasure. This causes great confusion in our lives, for we can never find enough of it.

We look for excitement outside of ourselves. We over eat, drink to excess, take drugs or indulge in our favourite activities to the extreme, all in the hope of feeling good. When we don't feel good, we believe that someone else must be at fault and not us, so we try and convince those others to fix the situation.

We want to be entertained, amused, to have nice things, to live in the lap of luxury, but our quest is never ending. As soon as we get something we want, we get sick of it and want some new thing to amuse us. We search for those high sounding aspirations like love, joy and peace but we never succeed in finding them for they are not emotions or commodities to acquire, they are states of being.

When our desire for pleasure is not forthcoming, we need to be consciously aware of that fact and nothing more, instead of identifying with it, as we all do, causing ourselves unnecessary pain. Our lesson is to learn to unconditionally accept life just as it is - which is a very difficult thing for us to do - for our emotions always get in the way.

When we desire things to be different from what they are, what happens is we get depressed, bored and impatient. So the more consciously aware we are of what we are feeling in any moment, without identifying with those feelings, the easier it will become to accept and enjoy life as it is – practice makes perfect.

There is nothing wrong with our desire for pleasurable things and feelings. Naturally we want to feel good, to feel better and be happy, but we are continually seeking in the wrong place, we are seeking outside of ourselves. It already exists within us – if we dare to look.

RECOGNITION:

Mankind is preparing to embark on a voyage to Mars. While there, our Astronauts are going to look for extraterrestrial life. But how will they recognize a Martian life form if it doesn't resemble in some way, life forms that we are already familiar with? If that alien life form is completely foreign to what they have ever seen before, how will they or the scientists back home recognize it?

They won't. As an example, when the British settlers famously sailed into Jamestown, Virginia, in the new world of America in the seventeenth century, the native Indians had never seen a sailing ship before. When they heard the sounds of the approaching armada, they did not see the ships in the bay because they were so alien to what the natives had ever seen before. It was only after the natives had numerous encounters with the ship's crew, did they finally see and recognize those large canoes with flapping white wings for what they were.

There is speculation amongst scientists about what type of life forms might be found on Mars. They expect to find only microbial life, if any, but even that microbial life will have to resemble in some way, the bacteria we already know about. If it doesn't, it will not be recognized as such.

If there is life on Mars, it may very well not resemble anything we have ever seen before, but even if it resembled say, a rock - would we recognize them as living creatures or think of them only as rocks, deciding in our earthly wisdom that Mars is barren and lifeless?

If any life forms found on Mars (or anywhere else in the universe for that matter) cannot be correlated against the life forms we are familiar with in our limited, earth based minds, Martians could be there right beside our astronauts and they wouldn't recognize them for what they were.

And if those Martians were of a completely different shape and form to us, but still as fully self aware and intelligent, they would probably not know the astronauts were there either, for we would be just as alien in shape and form to them as they would be to us.

COMMUMICATION:

Astronomers have been pointing radio telescopes towards the heavens for years, well before a voyage to Mars was feasible, listening for any sounds or messages from an alien intelligence. For instance, the Greenbank radio telescope in West Virginia, USA, is searching the heavens for ET, but what if ET has a completely different way of communicating than we have?

Will the scientists still be able to detect, recognize or understand the alien noise as an intelligent form of communication? Scientists may say, 'A sound is a sound is a sound.' But they can only form this hypothesis by how sound waves are interpreted by us here on Earth - which may be completely different to the way sounds are formed, communicated and transmitted by intelligent beings elsewhere in the universe.

What if the gold disc, containing music and greetings in 55 Earth languages that went into space with Voyager 2 in 1977 comes across an intelligence that is entirely different in its makeup to what we could ever understand at our present level, will they even recognize the space craft for what it is far less the little coloured disc with scribbles and static on it?

All of the monsters that ever were and still are depicted in horror movies, all of the creatures of science fiction, resemble in some form, life as we know it, whether animal, vegetable, mineral, insect or microscopic bacteria and viruses and they all communicate in ways that are somewhat similar to the ways we and all life on Earth communicate.

When we hear a sound that is completely alien to our ears - either it will not register, or it will be ignored. Anything, whether visual, audio, or from any of our other senses, can only be recognized by us when compared against what we already know from past experience.

The air waves could very well be chock-a-block full of alien life forms chattering merrily amongst themselves – or attempting to communicate with us and we would be completely oblivious of their existence.

REVOLUTION:

Nothing is more important to us right now than the evolution of our mind. The trouble is we have been going about evolving mentally in the wrong way - by thinking up ways to change ourselves. Thoughts can only make references to the past - what has worked for us and against us in the past that benefited our physical evolution only, ensuring our survival as a predatory animal.

The evolution of our species has been mostly a physical one and has largely unfolded unconsciously. Now our bodies have fully evolved, it's time to evolve mentally, but any change that we attempt through effort, which is the way we have done it in the past, is only ego effort, and our ego can never evolve mentally.

We can enlarge our police forces, march in protest, impose stricter penalties and create all the new laws we like – we will never get anywhere while we fight the symptoms of our problem instead of the cause, and that is just what we are doing. Not only are we not treating the cause, we are ignoring it completely.

In our ineptitude, we are trying to cultivate non violence by forcing people to obey laws, rules and regulations, but that is just another form of violence. We have done it that way for centuries and every time we have tried we have failed, for as soon as we bring about a new way of living it becomes oppressive and another revolution is needed.

If the world is violent, confused, self centred, it's simply because we are – the problem lies within us, not out there. A species that turns its violence on itself through revolution, is heading for self destruction.

The definition of revolution in the dictionary is: *'the act of revolving, or turning round on an axis or a centre; the motion of a body round a fixed point or line; rotation; as, the revolution of a wheel, of a top, of the earth on its axis, etc.'*

In other words, revolutions keep us spinning in the one spot, turning around and around in ever repeating circles without any advancement, always returning to the same place where we started. So it is with the revolution for change. We can never get anywhere but were we've been before.

REVELATION:

The evolution of the mind is an internal change that cannot come about by asking for it. The reason is that we simply don't know what to ask for. How do you ask for something you don't know? Change of mind can only occur through revelation, not revolution. This revelation has nothing to do with the mystical or the esoteric, but is something quite different.

Revelation is an inner sense of our need and urgency for change - to observe the need consciously and clearly without trying to bring it about. Revelation is the only way we can totally respond to the challenges confronting us today.

Our response must be new if it is to be successful. We cannot think about it and there is no authority that can advise us – for our own thoughts and advice from others can only come from the old and stale past, which has always failed us. We need to clearly see the problem we now face without trying to fix it. For that to happen though, something other than thought is needed.

The evolution of our mind is entirely up to us - personally. That may seem impossible and a bit scary for it is completely at odds with how we have tackled change in the past. We are used to relying on the group, society and outside authorities for the answers. This method will not work with the mind.

Only you can change your mind – *YOU* - no one else. That is our next evolutionary step and the miracle is, if one person can change - really change, it will be like lighting a candle. From that one flame, every candle in the world can be lit. That is the way true change occurs – personally – from person to person. Not from organization to organization, not from leader to disciple, but from person to person.

This must be done without trying to make it happen, but by simply being acutely aware of the necessity for change and the realization that we are quite capable of doing it. The ability has always been there within us.

SALVATION:

We cannot take any responsibility for or be obliged to assist anyone else to change. Our change of mind needs to be very selfish and yet selfless at the same time. The lifting of the veil of ignorance from our mind will automatically spread without any effort on our part to all humanity. We will have lighted the first candle. We have all that is needed right now, at this very moment for the evolution of our mind.

Unlike physical evolution, which requires the whole human species to change en masse on the outside – The evolution of the mind requires each human individual to personally change on the inside. Although the evolution of mind is a very personal one, as change spreads from person to person, the result will be a gradual and positive change in the way we view the world we live in.

At the moment we are going about it in the wrong way. We are trying to bring about the evolution of our mind using the old methods - by changing what's on the outside. We create rules, regulations, laws and penalties in a vain attempt to achieve this aim, which is doomed to failure, as we can plainly see in our world today.

We must seek an answer to our collective dilemma, each and every one of us, personally, for ourselves, without thinking about it, without asking anyone else – when the answer comes – as it will eventually, that is revelation – an instant recognition of the truth - a moment of inspiration.

The world outside won't change; it will be our attitude and the way we look at life that will change. We will be making the world we see a lot nicer, more peaceful and safer place to live. We will have consciously overcome our greatest hurdle and threat – our very selves.

It will be like living on another planet – 'A New Earth'. The evolution of our mind forecasts the evolution of the world – and the world is patiently waiting for its caretaker to graduate into adulthood and become masters of our own destiny.

RESPONSE-ABILITY:

Each one of us must take full responsibility for our own actions, we cannot afford to fail. We need to realize now, that the physical effort we have been using so far to try and resolve our problems has been largely ineffective. Our inadequate responses have caused our world to be in the violent state of anarchy that we now find it in.

Unawareness is the major handicap that is holding us back from evolving as competent, compassionate beings that are ready and able to take adult response-ability (the ability to respond adequately to the problems we now face) for the continuation and blossoming of our species in this world we have been privileged to inhabit.

Any physical effort, such as imposing restrictions and penalties or forcing others to comply with some law or dogma has not worked in the past and never will. To become consciously aware of ourselves at every single moment as we walk, talk and interact with people and the environment as a whole, whilst performing our mundane daily tasks is the solution.

A housewife needs to be aware of what she is doing while she is performing her home duties, a man at his work can stop for a moment and realize what he is doing. When walking, we can all become aware of the feel of the ground beneath our feet, the feel of our hands in our pockets, or the touch of the coffee cup. Although these actions may seem simple, they are important lessons that we need to learn.

Those simple tasks, when done consciously, change our whole day. Unconscious thoughts cannot creep up on us and take us by surprise if we remain awake and aware of the world around us and ourselves. We magically become response-able people.

We must become aware of our awareness, not be lost in our thoughts. Thoughts can be coloured by our emotions, awareness cannot. We human beings have a lot of good points as well as bad. We need to foster the good points while eliminating the bad, so it is up to each and every one of us to personally change ourselves within and save our species.

RELIGION:

Nothing has impeded the evolution of our mind more than religion has. There are many religious faiths and all are equally debilitating. For instance, when the Bible was written, the physical evolution of the human body was complete, except for a few tweaks here and there. This was all done unconsciously, by natural selection.

Our mind should have continued to evolve after physical evolution was complete, but so far it hasn't. It is still at the same stage of evolution as it was at the time of Moses. Our mental attitude and reactions to our world still triggers the same fight or flight unconscious violence.

The problem we have with religion does not lie with going to church – the problem arises when we believe in what is being preached. To believe what someone else thinks and believes, even if it is a large and authoritative religious institution, instead of looking within our own mind for answers stops us from self enquiry – hence, our mind stagnates.

Blind religious faith is a description that rings true. To have blind faith is to be handicapped. It stunts our mental growth. Religion is like a large mental block that has fallen across our way forward, pulling us up dead in our tracks. Not having the response-ability to work our way around the snag, we are stuck. We cannot move forward until we firstly become aware of the obstacle that is stopping us and then remove it.

We are like a flock of sheep, blindly following other dumb sheep as they rush headlong toward the cliff of ignorance. That is exactly what religious institutions want of course. Any follower that stops and thinks for them self would quickly see the hypocrisy of a religion that preaches compassion, love and understanding in one breath and wages bloody war and violence with the next.

The scriptures that we are asked to believe and worship took place centuries ago. The times of the Bible are dead and gone – they and the messages they hold, simply do not exist anymore – except in our antiquated belief system. We are worshipping a creed that is from the old, stale and dead past.

ARCHAIC IDOLS:

Supposing we were magically transported back to the times of the Bible, we would face a more hostile environment even than it is today. It would be as foreign as living on Mars. On the other hand, if Moses, Jesus, Abraham, Mohammed or any other dignitary of those times were to appear in the flesh today, they would be shot on the spot as being suspected terrorists or infidels.

Even if they had the chance to explain who they were, allowing that we could understand their ancient tongue, they would not be believed. Yet every week millions of us go to churches and temples all over our world and worship those ancient, archaic idols.

Religion is holding us back with an iron grip. It is as difficult to let go of as giving up oil driven machinery and coal fired power stations. Even if we are not believers and class ourselves as agnostic or atheist, we are still under the influence of a world that is dominated by religion.

Apart from mainstream religions there are the extremist cults and sects that have spread their idealism over our world like an infectious disease causing as much damage to the evolution of our mind as the plague did to our bodies.

To follow a belief system of any sort really is the blind leading the blind! The hypocrisy of a religious belief is blatantly obvious if we look at the anguish and butchery that religion has brought down upon us over its history with our eyes wide open and our mind in gear.

Both the East and the West preach virtues like forgiveness, compassion and understanding, but at the same time, anger and distrust flares between the two sides as the East accuses the West as being infidels, while the West accuses the East as being terrorists, causing unrest, violence and wars between the two that have been fought over the centuries and as we are still witnessing in the Middle East today.

All terrorism is carried out in the name of religion – my belief against yours. The West is just as guilty as the East. More human beings have been tortured and slaughtered in the name of religion than in any other form of violence - how immature and senseless is that?

IMAGINATION:

Consciously using the way our mind works can help us to think of alternatives to what we regard as reality. Imagine for a moment that our life consisted of everything that we ever wanted. We live in a beautiful dream house that has all the modern conveniences and appliances that we could ever hope for. We have the latest luxury car and all the modern technical gadgets that are available - money is no object.

We are lucky enough not to have suffered any kind of sickness, not even a sniffle and we can eat and enjoy any food or drink we wish as we do not have weight problems or hangovers. We have never been angry, unhappy or depressed - or indeed, experienced any negativity. Yes, we would be very fortunate.

We have heard on the grapevine about a land on the other side of the world that is reported to be the exact opposite of the one we enjoy – an environment where war and violence, poverty and crime, sickness, pain and sorrow are rampant. We are unable to even fathom what such a life would be like.

Living in this virtual paradise, we have grown used to the luxuries that are heaped upon us - in fact we have become quite complacent with our lifestyle and because we know no different, we find it difficult at times to fully appreciate what we do have.

We find ourselves wondering what it would be like if we lived for awhile in this reportedly hostile land.

What could we learn about ourselves? Would such an experience make us more appreciative of what we do have? We decide that the only way to find out is to go see. We know that we will always be able come back to this life of ease after our trip, or if the going gets too tough. So we set off to learn about ourselves on the discovery adventure of a lifetime.

Upon arriving, we are shocked as we descend into a negative, depressive environment such as we never thought possible. Immediately, we become embroiled in the pain and suffering of this strange land, which hits us like a sledge hammer. What have we got ourselves into?

APPRECIATION:

Originally, the plan was to simply experience this negative land and thus gain appreciation of the life we are eternally blessed with back home. Instead, we find that we have identified with this hell of a place as being our home, experiencing the ravages of hunger and thirst, crime and violence, hate and selfishness, sickness and disease - all the negativities we had only heard about before.

As time goes on, we get used to the battle for life and somewhat inured to the inner suffering that we now constantly feel. This life for us has quickly become commonplace. The memory of our life back home is pushed further and further back into the recesses of our mind until we forget the truth of who you really are and where we come from and where we will eventually return.

Not remembering the loving joy and peace of our homeland, we take what the locals here call pleasure and thrills as a substitute. Using these emotions, we find small comfort from the destitution that is now part of our everyday world. Eventually though, our self imposed life sentence must come to an end and we will be miraculously given the opportunity to return.

Upon arrival back home, we fully remember who we really are and with a sigh of relief, rush outside and kiss the ground in loving appreciation. We have returned from our escapade into hell, fully aware and unscathed. Asked by our loved ones what our experience was like, we surprisingly answer that it was the best thing that ever happened to us.

We now fully appreciate the wonderful life that is ours forever – and in fact, we will even consider returning to this harsh land on a regular basis to learn more about ourselves and to re-bolster our appreciation of what we eternally have. Although this is only an imaginary tale, it might serve as a contrast between what our earthly physical life experience and our eternal spiritual existence may be like. It's fun to imagine such a scenario anyway.

GUILT:

Strange isn't it, how our mind works? We have this ridiculous tendency to saddle ourselves with self imposed yokes of responsibility for any wrong that we believe we have inflicted on another, whether those others are aware of it or not. No matter if it's real or imagined this can bring about deep feelings of guilt.

Guilt can result from not saying or doing the right thing to another or falsely accepting responsibility for someone else's misfortune or problem. After the event we suffer feelings of loss and shame for not having said something or done enough to someone who is usually no longer around for us to apologize to.

Guilt makes us become over conscientious; we strive to 'right' the situation. We tend to 'over give' of ourselves. We are willing to do anything in an attempt to make everyone happy. We fret over every action we take as to its possible negative consequence to others, even if this means that we must ignore our own needs and wants.

Guilt requires memory to be able to function. The anguish of guilt is the result of what we have perceived to have done to someone else in the past. The incident that caused the guilt no longer exists, it is gone, it is part of what used to be, but our mind cannot let it go. We judge ourselves harshly, we feel remorse for our perceived misdeeds, and then we dwell on it constantly, causing ourselves unnecessary torment, for which we continue to suffer.

Guilt is an unconscious negative emotion that lives in past memories. We simply cannot be guilty in the present moment. We have to dwell on the memory of that incident to feel guilt. If truth be known the person that we feel guilty of wronging has moved on and forgotten the incident altogether – if they ever remembered it at all in the first place - and yet we cling to the pain.

It invades our mind like a cancer. All of this guilt is within our own mind, not out there or in the other person. What's done is done; we must learn to live in the present moment. If we can do that, the sickness of guilt will be miraculously cured.

BLAME:

Whenever anything untoward happens to us, we should try and stop for a moment if we can and turn the incident around full circle and pretend that we are the cause and that the unhappy incident that is occurring outside of us is only a symptom. We may be confronted by an angry person say, or an accident of some sort, a family squabble, or we're just having a bad day.

Usually when anything like this happens to us we blame the outside incident, the angry person, the other car, the wife, husband, son, daughter, the weather or just plain dumb luck. We tend to believe that what we experience in life arises from a complicated network of outside causes that we have to negotiate around every day of our lives.

We tend to attribute happiness or sadness for example, to single, individual sources. But if this were so, as soon as we come into contact with what we would consider to be good, we would automatically and immediately become happy and conversely, in the case of bad things, become invariably sad or angry.

The cause of our happiness and sorrow seems to be easy to identify and target. We tend to shy away from sorrow and chase after happiness. It all seems to be so very simple, thus we believe there is every good reason and justification for our anger against events we judge 'not good' and good reason for our attachment to anything that is pleasurable and good, but it doesn't seem to work that way.

A new approach is needed if we are to find continuing joy in our life, but how can we achieve that? As we have found, if we continue to blame outside influences for our unhappiness – or even our happiness – we are doomed to a life of chasing after dreams, that we then fear losing, instead, we must turn turtle and look in the other direction.

We must look within ourselves and by pretending just for a moment that we are the cause of our own unhappiness and the outside manifestation as only the symptom, we will eventually discover our own true and endless joy that has been lying dormant within us, waiting patiently for us to wake up to ourselves.

PERCEPTION:

Like a mirror, the world we see is merely a reflection of what we have determined as reality – the dominant ideas, wishes and emotions in our minds - That's how our mind works - we look inside first, decide the kind of world we want to see and then project that world outside, making it our reality. We are so close to ourselves that this is very difficult to see or understand this fact.

We do not see the world as it is – if it is at all. We see a perception of a world filtered through what we believe to be true. In other words, we make it true by our interpretations of what it is we are seeing - and we all see a different interpretation of the world that is unique to us.

Thus, the conundrum is: Is there really a world out there at all or only different interpretations of a world, perceived in our mind? Is the kind of world we experience outwardly, the same kind of world we are inwardly?

Everything we experience in the universe comes through our perception or takes place in our imagination - *everything*. All that we perceive to be scientific or logical or objective still comes through our senses and thoughts — people, places, events, dreams... *everything*!

How then can there be any validity to claims of the existence of a universe outside ourselves when we have no way of escaping our own limited viewpoint? How can we prove the existence of anything outside our mind without referring to our mind itself?

Can we prove the universe exists outside our perception of it? How can we be certain we even existed a year ago or a minute ago, or if we came into being just now with all our memories intact, how would we know?

When we aren't or thinking about something, does it still exist? If we're in a room, does anything outside that room exist? Do we bother to manifest that which we cannot perceive? Do the people in our life continue to exist when we aren't with them, or is our reality only what we're experiencing, right here, right now? Interesting how the mind works.

PROJECTION:

Our perceptions are created within our mind, over time building up a set of beliefs about what reality is, which then guides our attention, causing our eyes to search for those things that fit our pre-existing beliefs – projection makes perception - As a result, what we see is not reality at all but simply a mirror, a reflection of our state of mind.

We've been taught that we are a thinking physical being walking around in a material world. But is it possible that the material world is only a simulation that exists within our mind? What if the entire universe only consists of what we perceive right now in this very moment? What if outside of what we perceive lies nothing at all?

When we have a dream, are the characters in our dream conscious, or are they simply projections of our own mind? Why do we think our waking world is any different than our dream world? Why do we think one occurs in our mind and the other outside it? Is it possible that both are occurring within our mind?

How do we know any of the other people we encounter are actually conscious themselves and aren't just projections of our mind. Have we ever experienced anyone else's consciousness but our own? Are we perhaps the only conscious being that exists in our universe?

Is this assumption more or less valid than it is to conclude that all the other people we encounter are just as conscious as we are? Do we make this assumption when we dream? Why do we become tired the longer our waking world runs? Why do we need to sleep? What happens to our world when we are asleep?

It is difficult at times to fathom a plausible explanation of reality that we can fully understand. For instance, could it be possible that you have written this article yourself, because you are the only one that really exists and the author is only a perception in your mind? While in this physical world, will you ever know the answers?

EVOLUTION:

There is a restless churning within us – an instinctive impulse to learn something we don't as yet understand - an almost inaudible whisper on the winds of our mind that there is somewhere we are going that is very special - a position in the universe that is waiting patiently for us to mature enough to warrant the gift of the treasures that have been laid aside for us there.

This inner urge was there when we first looked out of the mouth of our caves and were blinded by the light of our first new day, making us instinctively cover our bushy brow with a hairy hand as we gazed out upon the breathtaking beauty of a majestic landscape that was to become our home. Mother Earth spread out before us like a living carpet. This was the beginning of our journey.

That same inner longing is still with us today. Its intensity has never waned over all that time but is relentlessly impelling us ever onward to a destiny that as yet we do not know. That inner momentum is evolution at work - the intuitive compulsion to experience and learn the new and unexperienced – the incessant spurring on by some inner force.

When we began our journey as primitive, savage beasts, physical evolution was first priority. We needed to survive in this alien world. Our bodies needed to adapt to enable us to successfully exist in a hostile environment full of other beasts that vied for our food, (that includes us as their food source) and shelter, essential if we were going to survive.

We were different to the other beasts in that we were blessed with a consciousness of self, albeit primitive. We were aware of ourselves as individual beings and as we evolved, we were also aware of our own impending and inevitable death. But that is where we have come to a mental pause.

Today it is imperative that we realize the urgency for our continued mental evolution. Our high-handed beliefs and selfish greed and materialism must be put aside for they are impediments to our success - obstructions that we can easily rid ourselves of if we really want to advance onward to where we are destined to go. It is up to us.

KARMA:

There is an old saying that has been past down to us from ancient times that is known as 'The Golden Rule' which goes like this: "Do unto others as you would have others do to you." How you treat your fellow man results in what is called karma. This advice is important for us to understand for it is essential if we are going to continue our growth and mental evolution.

Karma means the reciprocal or two-way relationship between us and others. In other words, the way we treat each other will either come back to bite us where it hurts or kiss us gently where it doesn't. If we treat someone badly, eventually we will be treated badly. The thief will be robbed, the rapist raped, the murderer murdered, the abuser abused etc.

If we could only wake up to the fact that whatever nastiness or torment we inflict on another, we will eventually bring down on ourselves and conversely, if we treat others with kindness, compassion and understanding, we will be treated accordingly. Every day, we are confronted with decisions to either be friendly with or unfriendly to someone. The consequences of how we respond, dire or not, falls back heavily on our shoulders.

We cannot do anything to free ourselves of karma, but we do have control over our actions that invoke karma. We can try and understand this by consciously observing ourselves whenever we interact with someone. A good habit, whilst the interaction is taking place, is to pretend that we are looking in a mirror. The way we treat them, is the way we are really treating ourselves.

We may become proficient at understanding karma's meaning intellectually but no matter how earnest we are, no matter how much we may see the necessity and urgency to change ourselves for the better, we all flounder on the shores of ignorance. To be consciously aware before we are about to hurt, chastise, ridicule, abuse or be un-nice to someone else in any way, is the solution, we then have the opportunity to see that the way we are about to treat them, could in time, impose a dreadful penalty on ourselves.

JUDGMENT:

Criticism of any sort blocks our capacity to be a more loving person. How can we truly love someone when, if they do something we don't like or *'against our better judgment'*, we automatically chastise them. Their penance is only ended when they make good their misdeed, then we may judge them as worthy of our love once again, though they are usually kept on parole for a time just in case they re-offend.

This same scenario is played out every day in families and relationships all over the world. If we are not being judged – we are judging others – either way, it is we who suffer. There is an old Spanish proverb which reads: "He who does not laugh at the faults of his loved ones does not love at all."

The prevailing tendency of a judgmental person is to constantly complain about and criticise others for their supposed indiscretions, imperfections or disabilities, which always rebounds upon the one doing the fault finding, not the one who is allegedly at fault.

As an example, a nagging wife will continually find fault with her henpecked husband. Surprisingly, this gives her a certain type of neurotic pleasure and power that she becomes addicted to and so, cannot give up. Her intentions appear on the surface to be admirable.

She may honestly believe that by moulding her husband into the type of person she believes would be better somehow than the way he is now would result in a happier marriage. Instead, she drowns any love they may have had in the past or may have in the future under a negative cloud of judgmental criticism.

She is her own worst enemy as she continues to nag her downtrodden husband. In reality, she is suffering far worse than him, as he can get away from her and go to the pub for instance, where she remains stuck with her own negative, complaining self, twenty four hours a day.

We not only have the tendency to judge each other, we more often tend to judge ourselves and everything around us, which spoils the spontaneity of life. We need to stop judging altogether and instead, learn to unconditionally accept whatever is in the vibrant, nonjudgmental present moment.

FREE WILL:

Perhaps the greatest gift that was ever given to us, one that continues to contribute to our growth and evolution today is free will. No matter how bad things get, no matter how dire our circumstances may become, we always have the free will to change ourselves for the better (or for the worse). This applies to us individually and collectively as a species.

We implement free will every day of our lives, but we are doing it largely unconsciously. While ever that is the case, we will never get anywhere as we can readily see in the world today. In our politics, in our economies and in our striving for peace in the world, selfishness, greed and violence are some of the unconscious, negative tools we prefer to use to try and get what we want.

By using free will unconsciously, we will always end up with negative results, which only exacerbates our problems rather than solving them, sending us around and around in ever repeating circles of despair. To use free will wisely, we must become consciously aware of our decision making so that our determinations are the right ones.

Every moment of our lives, free will confronts us with choices. Mostly it's mundane decisions such as what to have for dinner or what to wear to the social event, or where to go on holidays, but even those choices are made more wisely if we are awake and aware of what we are doing.

We will still make mistakes of course, that is to be expected, for we are still learning the ropes, but with conscious awareness of what is truly right and wrong; free will allows us to learn from those mistakes so as to make better choices next time.

We must become self aware when making decisions in life. It is up to each one of us to do this. We cannot put the responsibility onto anyone else. By consciously using our gift of free will, we will be able to steer our path around the negative pitfalls along the way and set a course towards where we are all eventually destined to go. How conscientious, determined and awake each of us is will determine how long it is before we get there.

FAITH:

Dictionaries define faith as, 'Trust and confidence in the truth, in honesty, friendship, and God?" As it is a great mistake to suppose that God is only concerned with religion, this same truth also applies to faith. The general belief that faith is something that has to do only with religion is incorrect.

Having faith can affect our whole outlook on life - constantly – not just on Sundays, but seven days a week. The only problem we have with faith is that we give it away to others, whether a person, a god or a religious creed. Faith is vital life energy and to give that precious commodity to someone or something else outside of ourselves saps our inner strength and stunts our spiritual growth.

True faith is trust in our own personal inner nature - God in physical form. True faith conjures up feelings of love, joy and peace – attributes of a consciously aware mind. It has nothing to do with any belief system, but simply a quiet and assuring faith in oneself and a knowing that all is well.

But we have come to confuse faith with being just a part of religion when in fact it is not. We profess to have faith in God, but that god is not the real deal, only a cardboard cut out manufactured by religious zealots to hoodwink the masses. Religion has usurped faith to suit its own purposes. Unlike religious faith, whose blind following keeps us in ignorance, true faith is an asset.

The real God does not want or expect us to kowtow to his every whim and impose penalties if we don't. Nor does the real God want us to die in religious wars or acts of terrorism fought supposedly in his name. These wars are waged for a false god, depending on who he is depicted to be and in what faith a particular mob follows.

Each denomination preaches that religious faith is okay – only if we believe in the same god that they believe in. But what happens if we don't? Faith goes out the window and we are classed as terrorists or infidels and ostracized to all but adherents of our own particular religious gang.

If we are in the right spot at the wrong time, we are likely to be shot for our 'misguided faith' as so many of our own kind already have. Millions upon millions of us have died in the name of religious faith and for that we all must share the blame, not just the perpetrators, for we are all collectively responsible for the world we live in.

Any alien civilization that may be watching us out there in space would be finding it completely unbelievable, and very difficult to reconcile the fact that a race of beings with the intelligence we have and the technical advancements that we have made could in their right mind be so homicidal, cruel and unkind to their own species as well as the other species that share their planet.

We certainly would not be invited to join up as members of a galactic community. We belittle our very own nature. There is not a different god for different religions, there is only one God that is an essential part of every one of us, so how can we possibly maim, kill or blow up another person when that same God resides in their mind as well as ours? - And yet we do.

There is no problem with a person who is religious, or has religious faith, or goes to church every Sunday

– as long as they think for themselves and are doing it consciously, not blindly following the doctrine of a particular religious creed, or because of the fear of punishment from a supposedly vindictive god. It appears that religion and religious faith are bad things to have - they are not - they are obstacles to be overcome by learning the true meaning of faith and God, and to do that, we need to have faith in ourselves.

THE EGO

WHAT exactly is the ego? That is a very difficult question to answer, for it is our ego itself that is trying to answer that question; a sticking point that is impossible to get away from, for to be a human being here on earth means by association, to be an ego. We accept the ego as being who we are, our body and our name, which is separate from all other ego body's and names.

Maybe though, it might be possible to sneak up on the ego and get a small glimpse of its true nature, something that the ego does not like, for it hates to be found out. It would much rather work unnoticed in the background.

The first revelation is that the ego, as a separate intelligent entity does not exist. It is a figment of our imagination. That is difficult to come to grips with because what we believe to be ourselves - the ego will protest saying, 'but I am me, look, I am alive.' In reality though, it is a phantom, a ghost who pretends to be real.

If it does not exist, how then can the ego protest? Because it is 'the real you', your true self that is under a hypnotic spell so to speak, not the ego that is protesting, supplying the intelligence attributed to the ego. We are of the mind and we confuse the mind with the ego but - the ego is not the mind and the mind is not of the ego. We have locked ourselves into a false identity crisis.

The ego is an integral part of the body, the machine we use to get around this physical world in. The egos workplace is the brain, that wrinkly clump of soft, spongy matter that's between our ears. Back in our caveman days, to survive the hostile physical environment that surrounded us, we had to learn a lot of things including what to eat and what not to eat - also how to kill and prepare meat from other life forms that supplied us with the protein we needed for our body to survive. We needed the ego to be able to succeed in doing that, but we don't need it so much now.

Our survival in those early days was facilitated by the ego that remembered the events from the past, which included all the food that was good and bad for us, so when we were hungry, the ego would sort through those past memories, (what nourished us, what killed us or made us sick and so on) so we would know what to eat and not eat, giving us a fair chance of surviving each day.

The same method was used to tell us how to protect ourselves from the environment. When the first cavemen got cold and wrapped an animal skin around their body, it was remembered, both individually and collectively. From then on, every time they felt cold, they remembered what to do for comfort and survival. In the heat, they knew from past memories to seek the shade or jump in a lake.

It's the same scenario for the use of fire, water supply and shelter, utensils and weapons. The ego's memory grew and improved the longer we inhabited this world. These memories for survival are passed down genetically to give our progeny the best chance of surviving physical life.

That is the one and only purpose for the ego, our very physical survival depends on it. Even today we need to remember how to get around in this world, to remember what to eat and not eat, to remember our name and the names and faces of all who are close, around and about us. Everything we normally do as part of the rote of daily living - all of this knowledge, learned from past experience is essential for our body's continuing survival.

So how did we stuff it up? We began by reliving memories from the past that we once enjoyed – and wanted to enjoy again. From memories that are essential for our physical survival, it morphed into an entertainment area. This idle activity was not necessary for our survival but as time passed, it became addictive.

As we got more proficient at it, we transposed those memories onto an imagined future, making things very complicated and confusing. Eventually the distinction blurred between our true life and the imagined life. We lost our identity and believed we were this false ego and the fantasy land it conjured up. It is now time to put our ego back in its rightful place and that is looking after our physical well being.

DESTINY:

Our lives appear on the surface to be happenstance, a set of random events that make up each day, but that is not so. There are no accidents, everything has a purpose. From the very beginning, our mind was provided with a set of tools, including free will that would allow us to learn from our mistakes and progress towards our ultimate destiny.

At the beginning, we had a lot to learn. Our physical evolution is doing okay, our body has adapted as our circumstances changed and will keep adapting as we go along - in that we have no control. Physical evolution is governed by natural selection, an automatic, physical adjustment to our ever changing influences and environment.

Mental evolution is different however. Although our mind has evolved over time to cope with our survival, it has now become our responsibility to continue its development. We are the only ones privy to the awareness of self behind our eyes and the secret thoughts that are churning around in that private space between our ears.

It is obvious that any substantial progress humanity might make must first be accomplished within ourselves. The fantastic thing is that although it is up to each one of us to change individually, if we can do that, the whole of humanity will benefit, for our minds are linked.

Physically, our basic body structure has changed in unison as our environment diversified, in other words, all human body's are synchronized. Even though some humans may have experienced different influences and conditions in different parts of the world, our bodies collectively, have adapted and evolved together.

It is the same with our mental evolution, only one of us needs to change for all of humankind to do the same. That is what evolution is all about. As our name 'Human Being' implies, we come in two parts, (a) Human and (b) Being.

Our 'Humanness' or physicality, has evolved as it should; now it is time for our 'Beingness' or mentality to catch up. We are privileged to have received this gift of life, for as human beings, our destiny is to play a vital role in the ever unfolding story of the universe.

"God is within you, so have faith in yourself."

THE TIME WARP

WHEN Columbus discovered America, he could have possibly introduced himself to the Native Indians by saying, "Hi, I'm an Eyetie from Italy." When Captain Cook discovered Australia, he could have possibly introduced himself to the Australian Aborigines by saying, "Hi, I'm a Pommy from England."

Both these men were right - in their own time and place. They were both explorers of our earthly backyard. They were representatives of known lands exploring and looking for new unknown lands and its local unknown native inhabitants.

Things started to go a bit 'warpy' though, when man went to the moon, our first foray to places other than our own backyard. So what did man do when he landed on the moon? He stuck the Stars and Stripes flag in the lunar soil and claimed it for NASA and America. Or that's the way it came across to most of us anyway. Not to say there was anything wrong with what particular country's flag was hoisted there.

If the Russians had got there first, it would have been a Russian flag, and the same goes if China or any other country had got there first. It would have been their flag flying in the lunar soil. We now know that there are no lunatics (on the moon anyway), but if there had have been, how would Neil Armstrong and Buzz Aldrin have introduced themselves. "Hi, we're Americans from NASA?"

When mankind first left earth's shores to explore the moon, it would have been more meaningful, logical and sensible to have had a flag representing earth to stick in the lunar soil. Our Astronaut/Cosmonaut representatives should have been trained by NASA or whomever; well before the Moon trip to introduce themselves to any possible, intelligent aliens that they may meet along the way, as Earthians from Planet Earth.

Up till now though, we have been caught up in what could be termed a 'Columbus-Cook Time Warp'. Man is stuck in the -20/21st Century. We still regard ourselves as localized to a particular country and creed on our little planet. We have neglected to advance mentally! We have managed to get away with it so far because the moon is only just over our back fence but now we are on the brink of journeying to Mars, a land far far away.

Man will maybe meet for the first time, inhabitants of another planet. So how are we going to introduce ourselves? By saying, "Hi, I'm an American - or Russian - or whatever from Earth? Wouldn't it be better to say, "Hi, Martians, we are Earthians?" What flag are we going to stick in the Martian soil? The Stars and Stripes - the Hammer and Sickle - the Union Jack? Do they represent mankind as a whole?

It's high time for Man to align with the times. We need to grow up. We can't stay stuck in the 'Columbus-Cook Time Warp' any longer. We are preparing to journey to another planet that lies well beyond our back fence. Our species needs to be properly represented if we are to explore the limitless cosmos. And that's a responsibility we all share, for it is *you* who is being represented.

To facilitate that, we need a flag that represents Earth to stick in that alien soil, one that we all can be proud of. Just as important is that our representatives hoist our planet's flag as proud Earthians. The basic mind set about us and our race must change. And that doesn't just mean for the Astronauts/Cosmonauts who are representing us, it also means us personally.

Essentially, you must change. An evolutionary change in the way mankind thinks of himself is way overdue. The time has come to reconsider yourself. We are all part of the one species that is about to embark on a journey into the great unknown, and before we do that, we must re-evaluate the way we determine ourselves, and how we are going to portray ourselves to the universe…

It is time for us all to rethink ourselves as:

> Firstly and most importantly is No. 1. Earthians.
> No 2. The country we come from.
> No 3. The state, region, province we live in.
> No 4. The city, town community etc. we call home.
> No's 2, 3 and 4 are already part of our nomenclature.

The exception is No 1. Who among us, when asked, "Who are you?" replies instinctively, "I am an Earthian." Of course none of us do.

But in truth we are!! It is the one thing that binds us all no matter what colour or creed. That's exactly the mind set we all must achieve if we are going to mature as a member of the cosmic community. Out there in the universe, to any inhabitant from another planet, we are indeed, Earthians, from a little blue planet far out in space, that's if our little blue dot is big enough for them to spot.

Once we begin the journey, we not only have the responsibility of representing ourselves favourably but also all the other living creatures that share our wonderful planet. Being the 'brainiest' of the bunch we have an obligation to Earth and all life on it. Sounds rather strange don't it? But we have always been Earthians. If we weren't, we'd be Aliens. We simply had no need to understand that while we have been confined to our own back yard.

Now we are preparing to venture well over our back fence into the cosmos. We urgently need to start planning, learning and changing our outlook before we embark. We need to design a flag representing our Home Planet. We all need to say instinctively, "I am an Earthian."

Why is it imperative that we do this? It's because the time has come for us to grow up as a species. We have graduated from kindergarten. We must move on to the next class - This time it's a universal class. For that, it's imperative that we unite as one and learn together. We need to be patriotic towards our planet - before our particular country, creed and beliefs.

Fighting between ourselves will need to ease up for us to be able to bond as one; as Earthians. We all need to start learning now. If we don't - Our species will be in big trouble. We are on the brink of becoming cosmic travellers; we need to change our mind about who we are.

"We are God hiding from himself, pretending to be us."

REFLEXIONS

THE FACE IN THE MIRROR:

If all of this is but a dream, if behind the facade of our human body we are truly an eternal spirit, a soul who knows all, an observer who quietly and unconditionally views the drama of our life, how can we ever come to realize who this 'observer' is, this 'one who knows' this awareness that is our essential and eternal self?

Go to the mirror. Look at your face. You will see someone who looks older than you looked several years ago, although inside you don't feel any older. This is because it is only your body that has aged. The timeless awareness through which you see your body is the one who knows. Your body is only a temporary cocoon for this awareness. It is a temporary and aging container for the undying consciousness of the one who knows - You.

THE TEACHER:

The answers come. We don't have a sense that I'm going to teach this person now. We find that teaching is spontaneous. We help people to step out of their identification with the unconsciousness self - with their basic human nature. This applies to everybody who is awakening, and we are all at some stage of awakening.

We are amazed when people come to us, people who are ready, and we find ourselves saying things that we previously didn't even know ourselves. It's only when the questions are asked, that we intuitively respond. As we teach, we learn. Realizations come. Teaching and learning means the same thing. We are here to help people go beyond their habitual human nature.

THE ROLE WE PLAY:

Imagine for a moment that you are dressed as a gorilla for a role in a play. A very strange thing happens though once you put on the gorilla costume – instead of maintaining your human identity – you firmly believe you really are a gorilla and so you live like one, sleeping in the trees, eating roots and leaves and madly thumping your chest.

You experience all the emotions of jungle life believing it's your reality, but eventually, as the final act approaches, you are on your death bed fearing that your life as a gorilla will end – which it does. Then you take off the gorilla costume and remember who you really are, a human being playing the part of a gorilla in a story about life in the jungle.

It's the same with your life story. You are dressed as an ego/body for your role in a play. When the final act ends and you die, you take off your human costume and remember who you really are, an eternal spirit/soul playing the part of a human being in a story about life on earth.

THE SUM OF ALL WE HAVE BEEN AND DONE:

In all our incarnations on earth, we are at all times the total of what we have been and done; what we have fought for and defended; what we have hated and loved. In the three dimensional consciousness of earth every atom of our physical body is a reflection of our soul - a crystallization of our individuality.

Our emotional and nervous structure, our mental abilities, our aptitudes, our aversions and preferences, our fears, our follies, our ambitions, our character are the sum of what we have done with our free will since it was given to us.

So every personality, the earthly cloak of an individual is different from every other personality. So we are different than others in our likes and dislikes, in our desires and dreams. Cause and effect likewise makes us different in our joys and sorrows, in our handicaps, our strengths, our weaknesses, our virtues and vices, our appreciation of beauty and also in our comprehension of the truth.

THE PURPOSE OF LIFE:

Unbeknownst to you, you have lived many lives in many bodies, knowing yourself by many names. Your life experiences go way back to even before the time you lived in caves and sat around camp fires dressed in animal skins. In your many lives since, you have experienced all of life's infinite variety as you struggled to learn how to survive, grow and prosper in this foreign, hostile world.

Each one of your many lifetimes was a stepping stone on your journey to where you are right now. You have done this countless times, advancing to the next level when you have learned and repeating life on the same level when you didn't. The whole purpose of your existence is to learn the lessons that are on your soul's agenda.

So what have you learnt so far this time? Do you feel confident that in your next lifetime you will advance as a more loving and understanding being, or do you have an uneasy feeling that you may very well have to repeat the same lessons again next lifetime?

BEYOND FACING OURSELVES:

If we didn't have the compulsion to appear successful, would we care if someone else was more prosperous and made more money than we do? If we had no attraction towards social functions, would it bother us if we didn't receive any invitations? If we were free from a dependency upon other people, would we be upset if they no longer wished to be our friend?

If our artificial needs fell away through self-awareness, would we need to be concerned about these things at all? No! If we face ourselves honestly, beneath the habitual mind and body - that false sense of self we call ourselves - we would find that something else exists within us that is basically awake as opposed to asleep.

We would find something intrinsically cheerful and free. That is to say, we don't have to pretend, it's just there, and always has been. We would discover that we are genuinely one-hundred-percent self worthy. We are essentially awake. We might think this is just an old myth, another trick to cheer us up. But no! It is real and it is good.

THE ILLUSION OF TIME AND SPACE:

Contrary to the way it appears to be, we do not travel through time or space, the illusion of time and space travels through us. The past never really occurred the future will never really arrive; it is all an illusion, an elaborate dream of the passing of time through space in an illusory, physical universe of matter.

We remain eternally motionless in the stillness of the present moment, imagining that we are living a lifetime, moving from an illusory here to an illusory there in a continuing illusory procession of onward moving moments of time.

None of it is real. Yesterday never happened, a moment ago never was, tomorrow will never be, it is all imagined moments of time being continually added to the memory banks of our 'physical information processor' in the human mind, giving us a feeling and experience of being a creature of form.

This is difficult for us to understand only because the wrong 'us' is trying to understand it. That 'us' is part of the same imagined drama being played out in virtual reality - an 'us' that we think existed yesterday and we believe will exist tomorrow. In reality we don't exist in this world at all - and never have, we are pure awareness, dreaming that we exist in a physical world of matter.

THREE ESSENTIALS:

Three vital ingredients are needed to create the physical universe – and yet they have no physical properties as such. They are each an essential part of our everyday life that we take for granted and yet we or the scientific establishment, are at a loss to define exactly what they are. They are Energy, Magnetism and Spirit. Without any one of them, the physical universe could not exist.

Energy - heat, electricity - has no physical properties and yet it is the power of the universe. Without it there would be no heat to ignite the stars into existence and allow living matter to evolve. Also there would be no light to show the universe was there. In other words, if it were possible for the universe to exist under such conditions, it would be freezing, lifeless and undetectable.

Magnetism – gravity - has no physical properties and yet it is the glue that binds the physical universe together. Without it, the universe would not have clumped in great big lumps of matter that enables energy to do its work. Instead, the universe would consist only of miniscule, sub atomic particles floating aimlessly about in a dark and lifeless, freezing void.

Spirit – soul - has no physical properties and yet it animates physical life and gives acknowledgment to the universe. Without it there would be no one there to witness that the universe existed, so what would be the point. There would be no logical reason for the universe with its energy and its magnetic attraction to exist, three everlasting, indestructible, essential, non-physical ingredients that enable our physical universe (and us) to exist.

WE ARE ALWAYS WHO WE REALLY ARE:

What or who is God? If he is not a singular super being, then is he a plural super being? If he doesn't live somewhere in the universe, might he be the universe itself and everything in it? If he does not have the same emotional needs as us humans, then does he have different ones - Or none at all?

God is not an entity, but rather a process, an energy. God is the Universe and everything in it - with no emotional attachments, no ego. God is a Non-Entity.

God is definitely not a He or a She, nor is He a being at all. Names and concepts are only used by us so we can attempt to get a grasp of the ungraspable.

God is Love and love is all there is. God is the Universal Loving, Intelligent Energy that is everywhere and yet nowhere at the same time. There is only an all pervading Omnipotent Intelligence that is neither as big as the universe nor as small as a pinhead nor anywhere in between.

We are God dreaming. The three dimensional world we see before us is not reality; it's an illusion within our Universal Mind. The dream allows God / us to experience and know our self in form and this can only be done in a three dimensional physical world made up of time and space and others. In reality God is everywhere. There is no 'place' where God is not.

We are unable to experience and know our self in our eternal, timeless home, where there is nothing else to compare us with but our Godly Self. We can only dream - a dream in which our soul remembers all our myriad mortal incarnations, but our human self can't.

YOU WILL NOT BE REMEMBERED:

Because you are so convinced you are real, you can't possibly imagine a life after death that does not include you as an essential part of it. The fear of you not being anymore is simply too terrifying to contemplate. But as unimaginable as it seems, you do not survive death – not as the 'you' you know yourself to be – for the truth is, you are not who you think you are.

Your separate name and individual self that you so protectively nurture, is in reality insignificant and totally dispensable, your human story so trivial, your survival or non-survival so unimportant, that you will not even be worth remembering once your life is over. What you do, how you act, whether you are good or bad or otherwise, matters not one iota in the scheme of things.

There is no condemnation, no penalties, no hell - and no heaven for you. You find that very confronting and inconceivable in your present state of mind, where you firmly believe you are so utterly important, but that is an illusion caused by your belief that you are real.

You simply can't bear to face the truth that you really don't exist at all, and never have – you are an illusion, an apparition in the mind of God. What is and does continue to exist is God, and only God, nothing else – and you are God.

The notion that 'you are God' doesn't sit well with your self perception, for to you, God is just another person, separate from the person that you are. This God that you are told you are is so far removed from your present idea of who you are, that you have not the courage nor the mental capability to even contemplate such a truth.

But you do continue forever - as God – not as you presently know yourself to be, and that thought deeply confuses you. You just can't comprehend the fact that someone else, supposedly out there or up there somewhere, a person you don't sense in any way as being you at all, is who you truly are, and not your pseudo self that is in this moment, trying so confusedly to understand it all.

A FOREIGN LAND:

Experiencing a lifetime as a human being is like traveling away from our home to a foreign land. Some things appear somewhat familiar but most are strange until we get used to them, especially conditions which are unappealing, thus unlikeable.

Our true home is a place of absolute peace, total joy and complete love. While we are living a life as a human being, we are separated from our home, and because our memory is dim, we can no longer be sure that these beautiful features will still be there when we return.

In the physical world we must learn to cope with intolerance, anger and sadness while searching for the joy and love we unconsciously miss so much. We must try and not lose our moral integrity along the way, sacrificing goodness for selfishness and assuming attitudes of either superiority or inferiority to those around us.

We know that living in an imperfect world such as this will help us to appreciate our home and the true meaning of perfection. We must realize that in reality we are perfect and learn to not take this physical life to seriously.

We should laugh at ourselves and the foolish predicaments we get into. Life is full of conflicts, and the struggle and the pain, as well as the happiness we experience are all reasons for our being here. Each moment we are learning something new.

We ask for courage and humility before our journey into another physical life. As we grow into awareness so will the quality of our existence improve. This is how we are tested. Passing this test is our destiny.

BECOME LIKE A CHILD:

We are born consciously knowing our perfection? So why does it so quickly become unconscious? Why doesn't that awareness continue? Why do we have to spend lifetimes struggling to rediscover how great we really are? We are not meant to lose that knowledge. We are born into this world with the full intention of holding onto it.

But somehow, something interferes with our well laid plans, our fears and survival instincts kick in, all sorts of distractions get in the way. We come into this world as babies with our magnificence intact, but we have been conditioned to forget it along the way. If we all remembered who we truly are, our lives would be very, very different.

When we look at very young children, they know they are special. They are full of joy. When you know that you are loved and special, you don't become selfish and egotistical – which is what the popular perception is. In fact it's the opposite, you become full of joy – the way you see little children who laugh so easily. This is what actually happens, you become like a child.

You laugh easily, you don't take things so seriously and you become a joy to be around. Actually you become much more giving. The more that you love yourself and the more you realize how powerful you are, you actually become much more generous because you can afford to be. You're not afraid. You don't keep things close to your chest, you don't compete or fight.

You know that you already have everything you could ever need. So you become very generous, giving, joyful and popular. People love people like that. So what happened to us along the way?

WE ARE VERY SPECIAL:

We human beings are destined for greatness – a place in the universe reserved just for us, but we have to earn our place first. In the past there was no great need to be aware of such knowledge, for we had other more basic tasks to learn, like how to survive, but not now. Now is the time of our reckoning.

We must become honest with ourselves and admit that all of our gallant attempts to rid the world of selfishness, greed, violence and terrorism, physical and sexual abuse, has done absolutely nothing to alleviate those problems. Why? It's because we are looking in the wrong place.

We believe that it is other people who commit those crimes, not us. But the truth is we are all *us*. If we can see any negativity at all out there in the world, then we must have that same negativity within us. The world we feel inside is the world we see outside. We have to be honest and brave enough to look inside our own mind and not out there, and realize our problems and the problems of the world lie within us.

We must cast aside our selfishness, greed and irritability and learn to acquire more positive feelings like loving compassion and understanding. This must be done without thought of reward like, 'if I do that I will become more spiritual' or, 'people will look up to me as being a better person than them'.

For us as human beings, the time has come. If we fail to take heed of our own inner voice, we risk self extinction and that will mean starting all over again. That would be a shame, for we as a species have put in a lot of great effort and done a lot of things right, as well as wrong.

We are very privileged to have been given this gift of life, so why waste it? We, as the most intelligent creature on this planet are destined to play a vital role in the ever unfolding story of the universe. We need to be ready.

OBLIVION

LOOKING at it logically, if this lifetime is it, the one time, one go at it, why bother? What would be the point of it? They say that, like with other animals, the survival of our species is only instinct - our inborn urge to survive, to suffer the ravages of sickness and disease maybe and the ups and downs of life in general before we descend forever into the depths of oblivion and our kids take over.

What a load of bullshit! If that was the case, once we kicked the bucket, what would it matter what happens on earth? We are forever unaware. We are not in control anymore. Our progeny, who follow us could very well blow up the entire planet for all we know causing the extinction of not only our species but the rest of life as well and what would it matter to us? What would have been the use of us putting in all the good work and trying to be upstanding citizens of earth? We are oblivious remember! We are *not* anymore.

Our experience of life logically must have a point to it, a reason, and a purpose. To have a onetime go at life and then be no more simply does not make any sense. We might as well forget all about progress and just whoop it up for the little time we are here if that be the case. That is not intelligent by any means - but the universe is.

It's common sense that our essential self does continue on eternally. The way that our mind works is in two parts. One is the ego, the driver behind the wheel and the other is the intelligence controlling the overall operation – our eternal true self, or soul.

The brain is not the mind so much as a part of the body, the grey 'matter,' sometimes called the 'habitual mind' which belongs to and is the abode of the ego, the person we think we are. When the body dies, the brain and the ego die too - by the way, that to the ego is a terrifying thought.

So really, total oblivion is preferable to the ego rather than have our true self/soul continue on regardless after our physical life ends, while the egos existence ends in oblivion - for the ego desperately wants eternity too.

PLAYING THE GAME OF LIFE:

Nothing can change in the spiritual domain in which God eternally exists, for there is no-thing there to change. God is not anywhere, at any time, for he does not exist in time and space. God is invisible, formless, intelligent energy that is everywhere yet nowhere.

In his essence, he is pure love, joy and peace. Thus he is eternally at peace within himself. But occasionally God wishes to reacquaint himself with being a finite form. Why? There is nothing else better for him to do. So he plays a game with himself

And that's where we come in. We are not playing God's game; we are an essential part of the game, like chess pieces if you will. We are God in disguise, who, for the duration of the game, has purposely forgotten who he really is, whilst he is disguised as us and everything else in the world.

We are the key. As the most intelligent of the species, it is us who must evolve and as a consequence God can then physically evolve. With free will, a gift God gave to himself at the beginning of the game, we all have the opportunity to seek for answers, wake up and fulfil God's wish, which is the reason for playing the game.

Most of us will remain oblivious of God's plan, but it only needs a few of us to seek the truth and eventually it will pay off, spreading to our fellow man. (The one lighted candle effect) Eventually, as our species evolves, mankind will be advanced enough to be able to handle the truth that we are really God in disguise.

Once we have done our job, God can then, through us, play his game while remaining fully conscious of who he really is and as a consequence, we can all consciously join in and play the game together.

Once the game is over, the world will end and God will resume his eternal rest, where he is at total peace with himself in a realm of love, joy and peace. Then there is a stirring within him, a curiosity to learn and experience more about himself in physical form - and then the game begins anew.

> " Should we then strive to awaken from the ego illusion and save the world? No! It's just a game, remember? "

EPILOGUE

YOU who are reading this book, do not realize just how privileged you really are. For a prerequisite to reading these lines, you need to be alive here on earth as a human being experiencing physical life. What an honour that is for you.

You could just as well have not been born at all and so remained oblivious to the life experience. Of course then that would not have mattered one iota because if you had never been, you could never have known or experienced the beauty of the life experience. The miracle is though, you are here experiencing life, so you do know.

Ask yourself 'why was I so special to have been given this gift of life from God?' How many billions of other seeds of life never make it, never get the chance to blossom, grow and take part in all the excitement and variety that life presents?

You are one of the lucky ones my friend. So the next time you feel downhearted, hard done by, angry with someone, or just with life in general, stop for a moment and realize that you have won the lottery, you are here and able to experience all the positive and negative stuff that life dishes out.

Then instead of an angry or despondent grimace, smile at the world and at life and joyfully exclaim, '*WOW!* I can't believe it, I'm alive, right here, right now.

❝ Be willing to start life anew every morning. ❞
